Table of Content

MW01233625

WELCOME ....

INTRODUCTION 6

CHAPTER 1: INSURANCE REGULATION...12

1.1 Overview of Insurance Regulation 12

1.2 Licensing of Professionals..12

1.3 Regulatory Authorities 13

1.4 Ethical and Legal Conduct 13

1.5 The Business of Insurance..14

1.6 Consumer Protection...14

1.7 Federal Regulations and Their Impact..14

1.8 Compliance and Enforcement..15

Review Questions and Key Takeaways..15

CHAPTER 2: FUNDAMENTALS OF GENERAL INSURANCE 16

2.1 General Insurance Concepts 16

2.2 Elements of Insurable Risks 16

2.3 Classification of Insurers 16

2.4 Insurance Producers and Agency Law 17

2.5 Principles of Insurance Contracts...17

2.6 Legal Interpretations and Contractual Provisions 18

CHAPTER 3: FUNDAMENTALS OF LIFE INSURANCE...........................21

3.1 Introduction to Life Insurance...21

3.2 Understanding Insurable Interest 21

3.3 Personal Applications of Life Insurance...21

3.4 Evaluating Personal Life Insurance Needs...22

3.5 Life Insurance in Business Context 22

3.6 Types of Life Insurance Policies 22

3.7 Premiums and Their Determination 23

3.8 Role and Duties of Insurance Producers..23

3.9 Underwriting Process in Life Insurance...23

3.10 Life Settlements..24

CHAPTER 4: TYPES OF LIFE INSURANCE COVERAGE 27

4.1 Overview of Life Insurance Policies 27

4.2 Term Life Insurance Varieties 27

4.3 Whole Life Insurance Options 28

4.4 Flexible Premium Policies 28

4.5 Specialized Life Insurance Policies 28

4.6 Group Life Insurance Framework 29

CHAPTER 5: UNDERSTANDING LIFE INSURANCE POLICY FEATURES, RIDERS, AND OPTIONS . 32

5.1 Introduction to Policy Provisions, Options, and Riders 32

5.2 Standard Policy Provisions 32

5.3 Beneficiary Designations and Clauses 33

5.4 Options for Settlement 33

5.5 Nonforfeiture Options 33

5.6 Policy Loans and Withdrawal Options 34

5.7 Options for Dividends 34

5.8 Disability Riders and Benefits 34

5.9 Accelerated Benefit Riders 34

5.10 Additional Insured Riders 34

5.11 Riders Affecting Death Benefit Amounts 35

CHAPTER 6: ESSENTIALS OF ANNUITIES 38

Introduction to Annuities 38

6.1 Basic Principles and Concepts of Annuities 38

6.2 Types of Annuities: Immediate vs. Deferred 38

6.3 Annuity Payment Options 39

6.4 Varieties of Annuity Products 39

6.5 Practical Applications of Annuities 39

6.6 Annuity Suitability 40

CHAPTER 7: FEDERAL TAX IMPLICATIONS FOR LIFE INSURANCE AND ANNUITIES 44

7.1 Overview of Tax Considerations 44

7.2 Tax Aspects of Personal Life Insurance 44

7.3 Modified Endowment Contracts (MECs) 45

7.4 Taxation of Non-Qualified Annuities 45

7.5 IRA Tax Considerations 45

7.6 Rollovers and Transfers 46

7.7 Section 1035 Exchanges 46

CHAPTER 8: UNDERSTANDING QUALIFIED PLANS 47

8.1 Overview of Qualified Plans 47

8.2 Key Requirements for Qualified Plans 47

8.3 Tax Implications for Qualified Plans..47

8.4 Types and Features of Qualified Plans 48

CHAPTER 9: FUNDAMENTALS OF HEALTH INSURANCE **51**

9.1 Introduction to Health Insurance..51

9.2 Understanding Health Insurance Perils..51

9.3 Types of Losses and Benefits 51

9.4 Health Insurance Policy Categories...52

9.5 Overview of Limited Health Policies 52

9.6 Common Health Insurance Exclusions...53

9.7 Responsibilities of Health Insurance Producers............................53

9.8 Individual Health Insurance Underwriting 53

9.9 Health Insurance Replacement Considerations 54

9.10 Mandated Provisions in Health Insurance.....................................54

CHAPTER 10: KEY PROVISIONS IN INDIVIDUAL HEALTH INSURANCE POLICIES **57**

10.1 Overview of Individual Health Insurance Policy Provisions 57

10.2 Mandatory Policy Provisions 57

10.3 Additional Contractual Provisions..58

10.4 Special Policy Provisions...59

10.5 Understanding Renewability and Cancellation Clauses................59

CHAPTER 11: DISABILITY INCOME AND RELATED INSURANCE **64**

11.1 Introduction to Disability Income Insurance 64

11.2 Eligibility for Disability Benefits...64

11.3 Features of Individual Disability Income Insurance 64

11.4 Underwriting of Individual Disability Insurance..........................65

11.5 Overview of Group Disability Income Insurance 65

11.6 Business Disability Insurance Concepts..65

11.7 Understanding Social Security Disability 66

11.8 Workers' Compensation and Disability 66

CHAPTER 12: OVERVIEW OF MEDICAL PLANS **70**

12.1 Introduction to Medical Plans...70

12.2 Understanding Health Insurance Perils 70

12.3 Types of Losses and Benefits...70

12.4 Health Insurance Policy Categories 71

12.5 Overview of Limited Health Policies 71

12.6 Common Health Insurance Exclusions 72

12.7 Responsibilities of Health Insurance Producers 72

12.8 Individual Health Insurance Underwriting 72

12.9 Health Insurance Replacement Considerations 73

12.10 Mandated Provisions in Health Insurance 73

CHAPTER 13: ESSENTIALS OF GROUP HEALTH INSURANCE **76**

13.1 Introduction to Group Health Insurance 76

13.2 Features of Group Insurance 76

13.3 Eligible Groups for Coverage 76

13.4 Marketing of Group Health Plans 77

13.5 Employer-Sponsored Group Health Plans 77

13.6 Small Employer Group Health Plans 77

13.7 Regulation of Group Health Insurance 77

13.8 Expanding on the Essentials 78

13.9 Advanced Considerations in Group Health Insurance 78

CHAPTER 14: FUNDAMENTALS OF DENTAL INSURANCE **81**

14.1 Introduction to Dental Insurance 81

14.2 Group Dental Expense Plans in the Workplace 83

CHAPTER 15: INSURANCE FOR SENIOR CITIZENS AND SPECIAL NEEDS INDIVIDUALS **87**

15.1 Understanding Medicare 87

15.2 Medicare Supplement Plans 88

15.3 Alternative Coverage for Medicare Beneficiaries 88

15.4 Long-Term Care Insurance 88

CHAPTER 16: FEDERAL TAX CONSIDERATIONS FOR HEALTH INSURANCE **92**

16.1 Introduction to Tax Considerations for Health Insurance 92

16.2 Tax Aspects of Personally-Owned Health Insurance 92

16.3 Employer-Provided Group Health Insurance Taxation 93

16.4 Business Disability Insurance Tax Implications 93

16.5 Implications of the Affordable Care Act (ACA) on Taxes 93

YOUR NEXT STEPS - EQUIPPING YOUR JOURNEY TO SUCCESS AND TAKING FLIGHT **97**

Welcome

Dear Reader,

First and foremost, I want to express my sincere gratitude for your trust in selecting this book. I understand that the journey towards passing your state life and health insurance exam is challenging and demands significant dedication and diligence. This is precisely why I've dedicated caI have also prepared additional content to bolster your exam preparation. At the end of the book, you will find a QR code. Scanning this code will grant you access to an exclusive set of 300 practice tests designed to closely mimic the structure and content of the actual exam. These tests are an invaluable resource, providing you with the opportunity to assess your knowledge and identify areas for improvement.

Recognizing the diverse nature of insurance laws and exams across different states, I have ensured that this guide addresses the fundamental concepts and regulations applicable nationwide, while also highlighting state-specific considerations where necessary. Industry-standard terminology is used throughout to familiarize you with the language you will encounter during your exam.

Your journey is important to me, which is why I've dedicated much time and effort to this book. If it helps you in your preparation, I kindly ask you to leave a review. Your feedback is not only a source of personal fulfillment for me but also serves as a guide for others embarking on this journey.

I wish you all the best in your studies and on your path to success in the life and health insurance industry.

With warm regards,

Fannie P. Abbot

Introduction

Welcome, aspiring insurance professionals!

Are you ready to embark on the exciting journey of becoming a licensed life and health insurance agent? This comprehensive study guide is your companion on the path to success. We understand the importance of passing your state licensing exams, and we're here to equip you with the knowledge, strategies, and resources you need to excel.

Why is passing the exams crucial?

A passing score on your state licensing exams unlocks a rewarding career in the dynamic world of insurance. You'll gain the ability to help individuals and families protect their financial well-being, navigate complex insurance products, and build a fulfilling career. This guide empowers you to confidently approach the exams and achieve your professional goals.

Overview of the Guide

This study guide is designed to be your one-stop shop for exam preparation. We've meticulously crafted each chapter to provide you with a clear understanding of the key concepts, essential formulas, and practical applications tested on the exams.

Here's what you can expect:

- Chapter-by-chapter breakdown: Each chapter delves into specific exam topics, offering in-depth explanations, practice problems, and relevant case studies.

- Succinct explanations: We present complex information in a clear and concise manner, making it easier to grasp and retain key concepts.

- 300 practice questions: Test your knowledge and identify areas needing improvement by scanning the QR code at the back of this book.

Understanding the Exams

If you want to pursue a career in life and health insurance sales, you will need to overcome some challenges first. The requirements to sell life and health insurance differ by state, but they all involve getting an insurance license. To get a license selling life and health insurance, you will need to do some research, show some dedication, and work hard, but it's not too hard to do it if you know how to get ready.

Before you apply for your health insurance license, you should learn about the exam requirements, how to maintain your license active, and how to pass on your first attempt. Becoming a licensed life and health insurance agent is achievable; just follow these steps to reach your goal.

Exam Requirements for Selling Life and Health Insurance

You need to register for the life and health insurance exams in each state where you want to sell insurance. So, the first step in learning about the exam requirements is to find out about your specific state. You can do this by looking for the department of insurance in each state where you plan to sell insurance.

The life and health insurance exam is one of the many topics that each state department of insurance will cover. The exam will test your knowledge of both types of insurance. If you pass the exam and meet other requirements, you will get your license and start selling policies. Other requirements to get a life and health insurance license include:

- Being at least 18 years old

- Having a high school diploma or equivalent

- Completing pre-licensing education hours, if your state requires it.

Content of life and health insurance exams

You should know the content of the life and health insurance exams before you take the actual test. The more you know the exam content, the easier it will be to prepare and pass the test. The life and health insurance exams will test your knowledge of various topics, including a general understanding of both types of insurance. Also, some specific topics you can expect on the life and health insurance exams are:

- Details of life and health insurance policies

- Annuities Tax issues related to life insurance, annuities, and health insurance

- Disability income Health Maintenance Organizations (HMOs)

- Policy riders that affect life insurance coverage

- Medical plans, including dental policies Individual insurance for special needs

While the core principles of insurance remain consistent, there may be slight variations in exam content based on state-specific regulations and coverage requirements. Familiarize yourself with any unique topics or nuances relevant to your state's exam. Each state will have its own state exam outline. You should print this out and use it as your study guide so you can review the content that you will need to know.

How To Pass Your Insurance Exams on the First Try

Now that you know what you need to do to get and keep a life and health insurance license, how do you approach the exam? The goal for anyone taking a life and health insurance license exam is to pass it on the first try, but that doesn't always happen. People who fail to pass it on the first try probably did not prepare well or understand what the exam would ask them. Let's see the format of the exam, as well as some tips and tricks on how to prepare effectively.

Format of the life and health insurance exam

The good thing about each state's life and health insurance exam is that you can pick a date and time. The scheduling options will depend on the state's department of insurance.

All testing is done on a computer, but you don't need any special computer skills to pass the exam. When you start the test, you can expect between 100 to 150 multiple-choice questions. The questions will vary depending on your state. Tests that combine life and health insurance tend to be longer.

Passing score and passing rate To pass each state life and health insurance exam, you will need to get a certain score. The passing score and passing rate will also vary depending on your state. You can find out the passing score and passing rate for your state by checking the state exam outline or the department of insurance website. Generally, you will need to get at least 70% of the questions right to pass the exam.

Demystifying the format and structure:

State licensing exams for life and health insurance typically consist of multiple-choice questions, with some exams incorporating true/false or fill-in-the-blank formats. The specific exam content and structure may vary slightly by state, so it's crucial to consult your state's insurance department for the latest information.

Study Advice

Embrace the power of practice:

Regular practice is the cornerstone of exam preparation. Use the 300 practice questions provided with this guide to identify your strengths and weaknesses. (See the Welcome page for access through a QR code). Actively work on areas that require improvement, and revisit challenging topics until they become clear.

Review and reinforce your learning:

Don't underestimate the power of spaced repetition. Regularly review key concepts, formulas, and important points to solidify your understanding and enhance long-term memory recall.

Develop a personalized study plan:

Create a study schedule that caters to your learning style and preferences. Allocate ample time for focused studying, incorporating breaks and self-care to avoid burnout.

Seek support and collaboration:

Connect with other exam candidates to form study groups, discuss challenging topics, and motivate each other. Consider seeking guidance from experienced insurance professionals or tutors for additional support.

Motivation and Encouragement

Remember, you are capable and prepared! This journey may seem challenging at times, but with dedication, perseverance, and the right resources, you can achieve your goal of passing the exams.

Stay focused on your aspirations: Visualize the rewarding career that awaits you upon successful completion of the exams. Let your passion for helping others and securing their financial well-being fuel your motivation.

Find inspiration in success stories: Surround yourself with positive affirmations and stories of individuals who have overcome similar challenges. Remember, many have walked this path before you and achieved success.

Believe in yourself: Self-doubt can be a hurdle. Trust in your abilities, the knowledge you've gained through this guide, and your unwavering commitment to your goals.

Practicalities

Taking the next steps:

Register for the exams: Contact your state's insurance department to obtain information on registration procedures, eligibility requirements, and deadlines.

Prepare for exam fees: Be aware of the associated costs for registration and testing, and factor them into your budgeting plan.

Scheduling and locations: Choose exam dates and locations that best suit your schedule and learning style. Some states offer computer-based testing, while others may have designated testing centers.

Understanding exam scores and results:

Scoring system: Familiarize yourself with the scoring criteria for your state's exams. This will help you gauge your performance and identify areas for improvement if necessary.

Passing the exams: Each state has its own minimum passing score requirement. Strive to exceed the minimum score to ensure a successful outcome.

Looking beyond the exams:

Continuing education: The insurance industry is constantly evolving. Stay updated on industry trends and regulatory changes through continuing education courses to maintain your license and professional knowledge.

A rewarding career path awaits!

We hope this comprehensive study guide will equip you with the knowledge, strategies, and motivation to excel in your state licensing exams and embark on a fulfilling career in life and health insurance. Remember, the hard work, dedication, and knowledge you gain on this journey will serve you well as you navigate the exciting world of insurance and help others achieve their financial security goals.

Chapter 1: Insurance Regulation

1.1 Overview of Insurance Regulation

Insurance regulation is the backbone of the industry, designed to safeguard policy-holders while ensuring the market's stability and fairness. This complex framework aims to balance the need for consumer protection against the operational demands of insurance firms. At the federal level, the focus is on maintaining the solvency of insurers, preventing systemic risks, and ensuring that companies adhere to ethical standards. Meanwhile, state regulations address the nitty-gritty of insurance operations, including policy details, pricing fairness, claims handling, and the rights of policyholders.

The National Association of Insurance Commissioners (NAIC) is instrumental in harmonizing these efforts, advocating for consistency and endorsing best practices among the states. Despite these efforts, substantial differences persist across state lines, affecting everything from policy rates to coverage options. Understanding these regulations' nuances is crucial for insurance professionals, enabling them to navigate varying legal landscapes and better serve their clients.

1.2 Licensing of Professionals

In the insurance world, the licensing of professionals is not merely a formality but a fundamental requirement to ensure that those in the field are qualified, knowledgeable, and adhere to high ethical standards. These regulations help maintain industry integrity, ensuring that agents and brokers possess a thorough understanding of insurance products, ethical selling practices, and state-specific legal guidelines.

Each state sets its licensing requirements and examination processes, covering different insurance domains such as life, health, property, and casualty insurance. These distinctions are crucial for specialists in each area to provide accurate, relevant advice. Moreover, states manage resident and non-resident licensing differently, imposing various conditions for license renewal, such as mandatory continuing education courses, to keep professionals updated on industry changes and ethical practices.

1.3 Regulatory Authorities

At the heart of insurance regulation are the state insurance departments, tasked with a broad array of responsibilities from licensing oversight to market conduct reviews. These bodies ensure that insurance practices meet state standards and that consumers' interests are protected. The role of the insurance commissioner is particularly significant, encompassing regulatory duties, consumer protection, and policy development.

While state authorities primarily drive regulation, federal policies also play a critical role, particularly concerning solvency and data protection standards. This dual-layer regulatory system ensures that insurance practices not only meet local needs but also align with national standards, providing a comprehensive regulatory environment.

1.4 Ethical and Legal Conduct

Ethics in insurance goes beyond mere compliance with laws; it encompasses the trust and fiduciary responsibilities agents hold towards their clients. State regulations enforce strict ethical guidelines, covering advertising, disclosure, and client interactions to prevent misleading practices and ensure that clients' interests are always front and center.

Violations of these ethical standards are taken seriously, with disciplinary measures that can severely impact a professional's career. These actions underscore the industry's commitment to maintaining trust and integrity, which are indispensable in the insurance landscape.

1.5 The Business of Insurance

Navigating the regulatory environment is a significant aspect of running an insurance business. Companies must comply with a myriad of rules governing everything from product offerings to financial reporting and market conduct. These regulations ensure that companies operate on a level playing field, emphasizing consumer protection and fair trade practices.

Moreover, the industry is under constant scrutiny to prevent unfair practices and ensure that fiduciaries uphold their duties. This regulatory pressure necessitates a culture of transparency and integrity within companies, fostering trust among consumers and stakeholders alike.

1.6 Consumer Protection

At its core, insurance regulation aims to protect consumers, ensuring they are treated fairly and can trust the industry. States implement a variety of measures to shield consumers from fraud, unethical practices, and exploitation. These measures not only provide avenues for complaint and redress but also enforce standards that prevent such issues from arising in the first place.

Privacy regulations, significantly shaped by federal laws like HIPAA, set strict guidelines on how personal information must be handled, further protecting consumers' rights and fostering confidence in the insurance process.

1.7 Federal Regulations and Their Impact

Federal regulations, while not directly governing every aspect of insurance, set essential standards that influence state laws and industry practices. Laws like the Fair Credit Reporting Act (FCRA) and HIPAA establish baseline requirements for privacy, consumer rights, and data security, which state regulations often build upon or adapt to fit local contexts.

These federal standards ensure a certain uniformity and protection level nationwide, guiding state regulations and shaping insurance company practices to better protect consumers and ensure market integrity.

1.8 Compliance and Enforcement

Ensuring compliance with these diverse regulations is a continuous challenge for insurance companies and professionals. States employ various methods, including audits and examinations, to monitor compliance and enforce laws. The consequences of non-compliance can be severe, ranging from financial penalties to restrictions on business operations, highlighting the importance of adherence to legal and ethical standards.

Review Questions and Key Takeaways

The complexity of insurance regulation requires thorough understanding and continuous learning. Questions such as "What is the role of the NAIC in harmonizing state insurance regulations?" or

"How do federal and state regulations interact in the insurance industry?" help solidify the concepts covered. This knowledge is not only crucial for passing state exams but also for professional practice, ensuring that insurance professionals can navigate the regulatory landscape effectively and ethically.

Chapter 2: Fundamentals of General Insurance

2.1 General Insurance Concepts

General insurance encompasses a wide array of non-life insurance policies, including automobile, property, and liability insurance. Understanding these concepts is crucial for identifying and mitigating potential financial risks. The cornerstone of this understanding involves key terms such as risk, which signifies the probability of a financial loss, and exposure, which measures the degree to which an asset or individual is at risk. Hazards, or conditions that increase the likelihood of a loss, and perils, specific events causing damage, are fundamental in evaluating and managing risk. Effective risk management employs strategies like avoidance, retention, sharing, reduction, and transfer, each playing a distinct role in handling potential losses and ensuring financial stability.

2.2 Elements of Insurable Risks

For a risk to be insurable, it must meet certain criteria, ensuring that insurance mechanisms can cover it effectively. These elements include the predictability of loss, which is enhanced by the law of large numbers—a statistical principle enabling insurers to estimate losses more accurately as the sample size of similar risk exposure increases. Adverse selection poses a challenge in the insurance industry, as those most likely to suffer a loss are often more inclined to purchase insurance, potentially skewing risk pools. Reinsurance acts as a risk management tool for insurers, allowing them to spread their exposure and stabilize the market by sharing large or volatile risks with other insurance entities.

2.3 Classification of Insurers

Insurers vary widely in structure and purpose, influencing their approach to coverage and customer service. Stock companies, driven by shareholder interests, contrast with mutual companies, which are owned by the policyholders and often return surplus funds in the form of dividends. Fraternal benefit societies and reciprocals provide niche market services, focusing on specific community or group needs. Lloyd's associations and risk retention groups cater to unique or high-risk areas not typically covered by traditional insurers. The categorization of insurers extends beyond structure to their operational scope—distinguishing between private and government entities—and their authorization status, crucial for ensuring legitimacy and financial security.

2.4 Insurance Producers and Agency Law

The relationship between insurers and insurance producers is governed by agency law, defining the legal boundaries and responsibilities within which agents and brokers operate. This relationship is critical, as producers act on behalf of insurers, guiding clients through the complexities of insurance coverage and claims. The extent of a producer's authority can significantly impact the underwriting process and customer satisfaction. Understanding these dynamics is essential for both insurance professionals and consumers to navigate the insurance process effectively.

2.5 Principles of Insurance Contracts

Insurance contracts are unique legal documents governed by principles designed to ensure fair and clear agreements between insured parties and insurers. These principles include offer and acceptance, establishing the mutual agreement; consideration, representing the premium and the promise of coverage; competent parties, capable of entering a legal contract; and legal purpose, ensuring the contract's objectives are lawful. The characteristics of insurance contracts, such as being contracts of adhesion and aleatory in nature, highlight the specialized nature of these agreements, tailored to balance the needs and obligations of both parties.

2.6 Legal Interpretations and Contractual Provisions

Interpreting insurance contracts involves navigating complex legal language and principles designed to protect the insured and ensure equitable resolution of claims. Ambiguities are typically resolved in favor of the insured, reflecting the contract's status as a document of adhesion. Principles such as indemnity and utmost good faith underpin the ethical and legal foundations of insurance, promoting transparency and trust. The implications of misrepresentations, warranties, and concealment are significant, affecting the enforceability of policies and the settlement of claims. Legal doctrines like waiver and estoppel are safeguards against unfair practices, ensuring that insurers honor their commitments under specific circumstances.

Case Study: Overcoming Challenges in Property Insurance Claim

Background:

ABC Manufacturing, a mid-sized company specializing in automotive parts, is located in an area prone to natural disasters. Despite comprehensive property insurance coverage, the company has never faced a significant peril until now.

Scenario:

A severe flood, categorized as a rare event in the region, severely damaged ABC Manufacturing's facilities, leading to substantial financial losses. The flood was identified as a covered peril under their property insurance policy.

Policy Details:

The policy included coverage for natural disasters, including floods, with specific limits and deductibles outlined for such events. It also featured clauses related to business interruption and the replacement costs of damaged assets.

Action Taken:

ABC Manufacturing promptly filed a claim detailing the damages incurred. They provided necessary documentation and cooperated fully with the insurance company's adjuster to assess the damages and determine the claim's validity and value.

Outcome:

After a thorough review, the insurance company approved the claim. ABC Manufacturing received compensation covering the repair costs for the damaged property and equipment, as well as financial support for business interruption during the recovery phase.

Conclusion:

Proper risk management strategies, including purchasing comprehensive insurance coverage, enabled ABC Manufacturing to navigate through the aftermath of the flood effectively. The incident underscored the importance of understanding policy details and maintaining open communication with the insurer.

Discussion Points for Insurance Exam Preparation:

- The role of risk assessment in obtaining appropriate property insurance coverage.
- The importance of understanding policy exclusions and limits, particularly concerning natural disasters.
- Strategies for documenting and reporting damages following a peril for insurance claims.
- The impact of business interruption coverage in mitigating the financial consequences of disasters.

Frequently Asked Questions:

1. What constitutes an 'insurable risk'?

An insurable risk must involve a loss that is definite, accidental, and significant enough to warrant insurance protection. It should also be part of a class of risks large enough to predict losses accurately.

2. How does reinsurance benefit insurance companies?

Reinsurance allows insurance companies to share their risk exposure with other insurers, reducing their potential losses and stabilizing their financial position, especially after significant claims.

3. What is the difference between stock and mutual insurance companies?

Stock insurance companies are owned by shareholders who expect a return on their investment, while mutual insurance companies are owned by their policyholders, who may receive dividends from the company's surplus.

4. Why are insurance contracts considered contracts of adhesion?

Insurance contracts are considered contracts of adhesion because they are prepared by the insurer and the insured has little to no ability to make changes. Ambiguities in the contract are typically interpreted in favor of the insured.

5. What does 'utmost good faith' mean in insurance?

Utmost good faith, or uberrima fides, is a legal principle requiring both parties in an insurance contract to act honestly and not mislead or withhold critical information from one another.

6. How do principles like indemnity and subrogation protect the insurance system?

Indemnity ensures that policyholders receive compensation for their losses without profiting from their insurance, while subrogation allows insurers to recover funds from third parties responsible for causing a loss. These principles help prevent financial abuse of the insurance system and keep premiums fair for all policyholders.

Chapter 3: Fundamentals of Life Insurance

3.1 Introduction to Life Insurance

Life insurance is an essential component of comprehensive financial planning, offering both security and reassurance. It represents a contract where the insurer commits to paying a predetermined amount to a nominated beneficiary upon the policyholder's death, in exchange for regular premium payments. This arrangement provides critical financial support to beneficiaries, mitigating the economic impact of the policyholder's death. Additionally, life insurance plays a pivotal role in estate planning, ensuring the preservation and transfer of wealth and addressing potential tax liabilities. Understanding the types and purposes of life insurance enables individuals to make informed decisions tailored to their personal and family needs, ensuring long-term financial security and legacy planning.

3.2 Understanding Insurable Interest

The principle of insurable interest is vital in life insurance, ensuring there is a legitimate, recognizable financial loss in the event of the insured's death. This legal doctrine prevents speculative practices and affirms that life insurance serves a genuine protective purpose. Insurable interest must exist at the time of policy inception and typically arises from financial relationships, such as those between family members or business partners. Understanding this concept is crucial for policyholders and beneficiaries alike, as it underpins the legal and ethical framework of life insurance, ensuring that policies are established based on legitimate protective needs rather than speculative motives.

3.3 Personal Applications of Life Insurance

Beyond its primary function of providing financial protection, life insurance serves various personal and strategic roles. It can be an essential tool for safeguarding a family's financial future, covering outstanding debts, and ensuring educational expenses are met. Life insurance can also be used creatively in financial planning, such as leveraging cash value policies for retirement income or funding charitable contributions. Understanding the multifaceted applications of life insurance enables individuals to tailor coverage to their unique life stages and financial objectives, ensuring that personal and familial needs are comprehensively addressed.

3.4 Evaluating Personal Life Insurance Needs

Assessing the appropriate level of life insurance coverage is a nuanced process that requires a thorough analysis of individual circumstances, financial objectives, and future obligations. Factors such as income replacement, debt obligations, and future educational costs must be considered to determine the necessary coverage amount. Techniques like the human life value and needs-based approaches provide frameworks for this assessment, helping individuals quantify their economic value to dependents and identify suitable coverage levels. This evaluation is crucial in crafting a life insurance strategy that aligns with personal goals and family needs, ensuring adequate protection and financial peace of mind.

3.5 Life Insurance in Business Context

Life insurance is also a critical tool in business planning, providing solutions for risk management, succession planning, and employee benefits. Key person insurance safeguards against the financial impact of losing a critical team member, while buy-sell agreements ensure smooth business transitions. Life insurance policies can also be structured to reward and retain top talent, aligning employee incentives with business objectives. Understanding these applications allows businesses to leverage life insurance strategically, enhancing operational stability and supporting long-term growth.

3.6 Types of Life Insurance Policies

Navigating the landscape of life insurance policies requires understanding the various products available and their respective features. From term life policies offering pure protection to permanent policies combining a death benefit with a savings component, each type serves different needs and preferences. Understanding the distinctions between group and individual policies, as well as the nuances of participating versus nonparticipating and fixed versus variable policies, enables consumers to choose options best suited to their risk tolerance, investment philosophy, and financial objectives.

3.7 Premiums and Their Determination

The determination of life insurance premiums involves a complex interplay of factors, including actuarial assessments, interest rate projections, and expense considerations. Understanding how premiums are calculated, the implications of different payment plans, and the options available for managing policy costs can help policyholders make informed decisions, optimizing their coverage and ensuring financial efficiency.

3.8 Role and Duties of Insurance Producers

Insurance producers play a crucial role in the life insurance ecosystem, serving as the primary interface between insurers and consumers. Their responsibilities extend beyond sales, encompassing client education, policy customization, and ongoing service. Adherence to ethical standards and regulatory requirements is essential, ensuring that consumers are provided with accurate information and suitable recommendations. Understanding the role and expectations of insurance producers enhances the purchasing process, ensuring that policyholders receive valuable guidance and support.

3.9 Underwriting Process in Life Insurance

The underwriting process is central to life insurance, assessing the risk profile of applicants to determine policy terms and premiums. This evaluation includes medical, lifestyle, and financial assessments, contributing to a fair and accurate risk classification. Understanding this process helps applicants prepare for underwriting inquiries and facilitates smoother policy issuance.

3.10 Life Settlements

Life settlements represent an alternative for policyholders, allowing them to sell their policies for immediate financial benefit. This option can be particularly valuable for those facing changed circumstances or who no longer require the original coverage. Understanding life settlements provides policyholders with additional flexibility, enabling informed decisions about managing existing life insurance policies.

Remember, practice exam questions related to "Fundamentals

Case Study: Navigating Life Insurance for Estate Planning

Background:

Ali Kahn, a 65-year-old retired businessman, has a complex estate plan and wants to ensure that his wealth is passed on to his children and grandchildren without significant tax burdens.

Scenario:

Ali holds various assets, including real estate, stocks, and retirement accounts. He is concerned about the potential tax implications for his heirs and seeks a strategy to mitigate these while providing for his wife's future financial security.

Policy Details:

After consulting with his financial advisor, Ali decides to purchase a universal life insurance policy with a death benefit large enough to cover potential estate taxes and provide additional support to his family.

Action Taken:

Ali works with his insurance agent to set up the policy, ensuring it is owned by an irrevocable life insurance trust (ILIT) to keep the proceeds outside his taxable estate.

Outcome: Upon Ali's passing, the life insurance policy pays out to the ILIT, providing tax-free funds to cover estate taxes and support his wife and heirs as per the trust's instructions.

Conclusion: Proper planning and understanding of life insurance's role in estate management allowed Ali to safeguard his assets and ensure a smoother wealth transfer to his beneficiaries.

Discussion Points for Insurance Exam Preparation:

- The importance of insurable interest in setting up a life insurance policy for estate planning.
- How life insurance proceeds can be used to cover estate taxes and protect beneficiaries' inheritances.
- The role of trusts in managing life insurance proceeds for estate planning purposes.

Frequently Asked Questions:

1. What is the principle of insurable interest, and why is it important in life insurance?

Insurable interest exists when the policyholder stands to suffer a financial loss from the insured's death. It is crucial to prevent insurance fraud and ensure that life insurance serves its intended purpose of financial protection.

2. How do different life insurance policies cater to varying personal and business needs?

Term life insurance offers pure death benefit protection for a specified period, suitable for temporary needs. In contrast, whole life and universal life policies provide lifelong coverage and can accumulate cash value, serving longer-term financial planning and business strategies.

3. Can life insurance be used for charitable giving?

Yes, life insurance can be an effective tool for charitable giving, either by naming a charity as a beneficiary or using the cash value of a policy to fund charitable donations, potentially providing tax benefits and fulfilling philanthropic goals.

4. What factors should be considered when assessing personal life insurance needs?

Considerations include current and future financial obligations, income replacement needs, estate planning goals, and the potential need for liquidity or wealth transfer strategies.

5. How does the underwriting process affect life insurance policy issuance and premiums?

The underwriting process assesses the risk associated with insuring an individual based on health, lifestyle, and financial factors. This assessment determines eligibility and premium rates, with higher risks leading to higher premiums or potential coverage limitations.

6. What are life settlements, and when might they be a viable option for policyholders?

Life settlements involve selling a life insurance policy to a third party for more than its cash surrender value but less than its net death benefit. They can be a viable option for policyholders who no longer need the coverage, face financial hardships, or wish to access the policy's value for other needs.

Chapter 4: Types of Life Insurance Coverage

4.1 Overview of Life Insurance Policies

Life insurance stands as a fundamental pillar in ensuring financial security and providing peace of mind for individuals and their families. Understanding the diverse array of life insurance policies available is critical for individuals looking to align insurance coverage with their unique financial and personal objectives. The array of life insurance options caters to a variety of needs, from temporary coverage for specific financial responsibilities to lifelong protection and wealth accumulation. By comprehensively understanding the distinctions and benefits of each type of policy, individuals can make informed decisions that provide optimal coverage and financial assurance for themselves and their loved ones.

4.2 Term Life Insurance Varieties

Term life insurance is designed to offer financial protection for a predetermined period, making it a suitable choice for those seeking straightforward, cost-effective coverage. Level Term policies provide the security of fixed premiums and a constant death benefit, offering predictability and stability for the policy duration. Annual Renewable Term policies afford the flexibility of yearly renewals but with premiums that typically increase with age, reflecting the rising cost of insurance. Level Premium Term policies combine the benefits of term coverage with fixed payments, often extending up to 20 or 30 years, providing long-term security with predictable costs. Decreasing Term insurance, commonly associated with mortgage protection, sees the coverage amount diminish over time, mirroring the decrease in outstanding debt, making it an efficient option for those focused on covering specific financial obligations.

4.3 Whole Life Insurance Options

Whole Life Insurance provides a comprehensive solution, offering lifelong protection alongside an investment component known as cash value, which grows over time. Continuous Premium (Straight Life) policies require ongoing payments, generally for the policyholder's lifetime, fostering cash value growth and enduring protection. Limited Payment policies offer an alternative by allowing policyholders to complete premium payments within a specified timeframe, such as 20 years or until age 65, after which coverage continues without further payments. Single Premium Whole Life presents an immediate, fully funded policy through a single lump-sum payment, providing instant cash value and lifelong coverage, making it an attractive option for those seeking immediate benefits and long-term security.

4.4 Flexible Premium Policies

Universal Life Insurance stands out for its adaptability, providing policyholders with the ability to adjust premiums and death benefits according to their changing financial circumstances. This type of policy not only offers flexible payment options but also the potential for cash value growth, subject to current interest rates and market conditions. The adjustable nature of Universal Life Insurance ensures that policyholders can respond to life's uncertainties and financial changes, making it a preferred choice for those seeking both protection and flexibility in their financial planning.

4.5 Specialized Life Insurance Policies

Specialized life insurance policies, such as Joint Life and Survivorship Life, cater to specific planning needs, particularly in the realm of estate planning and tax management. Joint Life Insurance, paying out on the first death, is often used by couples looking to provide immediate financial support to the surviving partner. In contrast, Survivorship Life Insurance, paying after both insured parties have passed, serves as a strategic tool for estate planning, aiming to preserve wealth for heirs or settle estate taxes efficiently.

4.6 Group Life Insurance Framework

Group Life Insurance provides a valuable benefit through employers, associations, or other group entities, enabling coverage for a large number of individuals under a single policy. This collective approach to life insurance offers the advantages of simplified underwriting and, often, lower premium rates compared to individual policies. Furthermore, group life insurance often includes conversion rights, allowing individuals to transition to personal policies upon leaving the group, ensuring continued protection. Understanding the nuances of group coverage, including the conditions for maintaining or converting coverage, is crucial for individuals as they navigate life changes and employment transitions.

Case Study: Maximizing Benefits: The Johnson Family's Life Insurance Strategy

Background:

The Johnson family consists of two parents and three children. They are considering life insurance policies to secure their financial future and provide for any unforeseen circumstances.

Scenario:

The Johnsons are assessing their life insurance needs to cover their mortgage, children's education, and provide income replacement in the event of a tragedy.

Policy Details:

The family is considering a mix of term and whole life policies. The parents are looking at 20-year level term life insurance to cover the mortgage and educational expenses. Additionally, they are exploring whole life policies for long-term financial stability and wealth transfer.

Action Taken:

After consulting with a financial advisor, the Johnsons decide to purchase a $500,000 20-year level term policy for each parent to cover immediate financial obligations and a $250,000 whole life policy for each to ensure lifelong coverage and cash value accumulation.

Outcome:

The term life policies provide a safety net for the family's immediate needs, while the whole life policies contribute to their long-term financial goals and estate planning.

Conclusion:

By combining term and whole life insurance, the Johnson family effectively addresses both their short-term needs and long-term objectives, ensuring comprehensive financial protection.

Discussion Points for Insurance Exam Preparation:

- The importance of assessing short-term and long-term financial needs when choosing life insurance.

- The benefits and limitations of term versus whole life insurance.

- Strategies for integrating various types of life insurance into comprehensive financial planning.

Frequently Asked Questions:

1. What are the key differences between term and whole life insurance?

Term life insurance provides coverage for a specific period and pays out only if the insured dies during that term. Whole life insurance provides lifelong coverage and includes a cash value component that grows over time.

2. How can life insurance be used as part of estate planning?

Life insurance can help cover estate taxes, provide for heirs, and ensure that other assets are not liquidated under unfavorable conditions. It can also be used to equalize inheritances among multiple beneficiaries.

3. What is the significance of having an 'insurable interest' in life insurance?

Insurable interest is required to purchase a life insurance policy on someone's life. It means the policyholder would suffer a financial loss or certain hardships in the event of the insured's death.

4. Can you convert a term life insurance policy into a whole life policy?

Many term life policies include a conversion rider that allows the policyholder to convert the policy into a whole life or universal life policy without undergoing additional medical underwriting.

5. What factors affect life insurance premium costs?

Factors include the type of policy, the insured's age, health, lifestyle, and the amount of coverage. For term policies, the length of the term also affects premiums.

6. Why might someone choose universal life insurance over other types?

Universal life insurance offers flexible premiums and death benefits, which can be adjusted over time to fit changing financial circumstances, making it a suitable option for those seeking both insurance protection and savings growth.

Chapter 5: Understanding Life Insurance Policy Features, Riders, and Options

5.1 Introduction to Policy Provisions, Options, and Riders

Life insurance policies are comprehensive contracts filled with various clauses and stipulations crucial to the policy's functioning and the policyholder's rights. These documents outline the terms of the agreement between the insurer and the insured, detailing obligations, benefits, and options. Understanding these elements is vital for policyholders to manage their policies effectively and ensure alignment with their financial and familial objectives. Familiarity with the provisions, options, and riders can significantly impact financial planning, enabling policyholders to utilize their life insurance policies to their fullest potential.

5.2 Standard Policy Provisions

Life insurance contracts incorporate several key provisions affecting control, payments, and the terms of the agreement. Ownership defines who has authority over the policy, influencing decisions like beneficiary designation and policy loans. Assignment involves transferring these rights, affecting control and benefits. The Entire Contract clause underscores that the policy and its applications are the binding agreement, emphasizing the importance of accuracy and completeness in application answers. Modifications clarify that changes to the policy must be officially endorsed by the insurer to take effect, maintaining contractual integrity. The Free Look Period offers a risk-free evaluation time, allowing policyholders to reconsider their investment. Premium Payment guidelines are critical for maintaining coverage, stipulating the when and how of payments. The Grace Period and Reinstatement provisions offer safety nets for maintaining coverage even after lapses, under specific conditions. The Incontestability clause provides a timeframe beyond which the insurer cannot challenge the policy's validity, enhancing consumer protection. Misstatement of Age or Sex and policy Exclusions clarify coverage adjustments and limitations, respectively, ensuring clear expectations. Interest on Delayed Benefits addresses compensation for late payment of claims, protecting beneficiaries financially.

5.3 Beneficiary Designations and Clauses

Designating a beneficiary is a critical element of life insurance planning, directing who will receive the policy's benefits. This choice can encompass individuals, legal entities, or trusts, reflecting the policyholder's wishes and financial strategies. Succession rules and revocable versus irrevocable designations offer flexibility and security in determining beneficiaries. The Common Disaster Clause and Spendthrift Clause provide solutions for specific scenarios, safeguarding the intended distribution of benefits and protecting them from creditors, ensuring that the policy's proceeds achieve the policyholder's objectives effectively.

5.4 Options for Settlement

Settlement options provide beneficiaries with choices on how they receive the death benefits, ranging from lump-sum payments to ongoing income streams, accommodating different financial needs and planning goals. Interest Only, Fixed-Period, and Fixed-Amount Installments offer varying payout structures, while Life Income options provide lifetime financial support, reflecting varied beneficiary needs. Understanding these options allows beneficiaries to make informed decisions that best suit their circumstances and financial planning requirements.

5.5 Nonforfeiture Options

Nonforfeiture options protect policyholders' interests if a policy lapses due to unpaid premiums, offering alternatives like Cash Surrender Value or Reduced Paid-Up Insurance. These options ensure that the policyholder retains some value from their policy, reflecting the premiums already paid, providing a safety net and preserving financial value even when full coverage is no longer feasible or desired.

5.6 Policy Loans and Withdrawal Options

Life insurance policies with cash value offer financial flexibility through Policy Loans and Withdrawal Options, allowing policyholders to access funds for immediate needs without forfeiting coverage. These features can be instrumental in financial emergencies, offering an alternative source of funds while maintaining the insurance safety net.

5.7 Options for Dividends

For participating policies, Dividends represent a share of the insurer's surplus, returned to policyholders in various forms such as Cash Payments or Paid-Up Additions. These dividends can enhance the policy's value or reduce out-of-pocket expenses, contributing to the policy's flexibility and growth potential.

5.8 Disability Riders and Benefits

Disability Riders, including Waiver of Premium and Disability Income Benefits, offer protection against financial strain during periods of disability, ensuring that the policyholder's coverage continues or that they receive a steady income, providing crucial support during challenging times.

5.9 Accelerated Benefit Riders

Accelerated Benefit Riders allow policyholders facing terminal illnesses to access part of their death benefit early, offering financial relief when it's most needed, although reducing the eventual payout to beneficiaries.

5.10 Additional Insured Riders

These riders extend coverage within a single policy to additional insureds, such as family members, optimizing coverage and consolidating insurance needs into one policy framework, providing a streamlined approach to family life insurance planning.

5.11 Riders Affecting Death Benefit Amounts

Riders like Accidental Death and Cost of Living adjustments provide additional layers of protection and adaptability to the life insurance policy, catering to specific needs or responding to changing economic conditions, enhancing the policy's responsiveness and relevance to the policyholder's life stages and circumstances.

Case Study Title: Navigating Family Protection with Comprehensive Life Insurance

Background:

The Thompson family consists of two working parents and two young children. They are exploring life insurance options to ensure financial security for their family's future.

Scenario:

Both parents want to ensure that their children's needs, such as education and living expenses, are met in the event of their untimely deaths. They also want to build a cash value for future needs.

Policy Details:

The Thompsons decide on a combination of whole life and term insurance policies, with added riders to enhance coverage. They choose a joint life policy for immediate financial support upon the first death and a survivorship policy aimed at estate planning and wealth transfer.

Action Taken:

They include riders such as Waiver of Premium, Accidental Death, and Child Term Riders, ensuring that their coverage adapts to various unforeseen circumstances.

Outcome:

The comprehensive coverage provides peace of mind, knowing that immediate and future financial needs are addressed. The cash value component grows, offering financial flexibility.

Conclusion:

By carefully selecting policies and riders, the Thompson family effectively tailors their life insurance to meet both current and future needs, ensuring holistic protection.

Discussion Points for Insurance Exam Preparation:

- Importance of combining different types of life insurance policies to meet diverse needs.
- The role and impact of various riders in enhancing insurance coverage.
- Strategies for balancing immediate financial protection with long-term wealth building.

Frequently Asked Questions:

1. What is the purpose of the Waiver of Premium rider in life insurance?

This rider waives the policyholder's premium payments if they become disabled, ensuring the policy remains in force during the disability period.

2. How does the Accidental Death Benefit rider work?

It provides an additional death benefit amount if the insured's death is due to an accident, offering extra financial protection.

3. Can a life insurance policy have multiple beneficiaries?

Yes, policyholders can name multiple beneficiaries and specify the percentage of the death benefit each receives.

4. What is the benefit of adding a Child Term Rider?

It extends coverage to the insured's children, providing them with life insurance protection without needing separate policies.

5. How does the Cash Surrender Value in a life insurance policy function?

It represents the amount the policyholder can receive if they surrender the policy before death, derived from the policy's cash value minus any surrender charges.

6. What are Nonforfeiture Options in a life insurance policy?

These options allow policyholders to receive benefits from their policy even if it lapses due to unpaid premiums, such as taking the cash value or converting to extended term or reduced paid-up insurance.

Chapter 6: Essentials of Annuities

Introduction to Annuities

Annuities are pivotal financial tools designed to provide a stable income stream, particularly crucial during retirement. They serve as a cornerstone for retirement planning, ensuring individuals can maintain a comfortable lifestyle without the fear of outliving their savings. By converting a lump sum into a series of payments, annuities provide financial security and predictability, supporting retirees in managing their income effectively. Understanding the role and functionality of annuities is essential for anyone looking to secure their financial future, especially as they transition from accumulation to distribution phases in their financial lifecycle.

6.1 Basic Principles and Concepts of Annuities

The foundational principles of annuities rest on the concepts of risk management and income sustainability. Annuities are structured around the Accumulation and Annuity phases, offering a unique blend of investment and insurance to cater to long-term financial needs. The contract owner, annuitant, and beneficiary play distinct roles in the annuity contract, shaping the policy's structure and outcomes. This dual nature of annuities, encompassing both the growth of funds and their eventual distribution, makes them an indispensable tool in financial and retirement planning, providing a safeguard against the risk of longevity and market volatility.

6.2 Types of Annuities: Immediate vs. Deferred

Understanding the distinction between Immediate and Deferred Annuities is crucial for effective retirement planning. Immediate Annuities offer immediate returns on investment, ideal for those at or near retirement age seeking consistent income streams. In contrast, Deferred Annuities are suited for long-term growth, allowing investments to compound over time before initiating payouts. Each type caters to different stages of financial planning, with varying implications for estate planning, tax liability, and income continuity. The choice between immediate and deferred annuities hinges on individual financial situations, goals, and the timing of income needs.

6.3 Annuity Payment Options

The flexibility in annuity payment options allows for tailored financial strategies to meet individual income needs and objectives. From ensuring lifetime income to protecting financial legacies, the variety of payout options — including Pure Life and Joint Life policies — cater to diverse financial situations and planning goals. The selection process involves balancing longevity risks with financial needs and preferences, ensuring that retirees can optimize their income streams based on personal circumstances and market conditions.

6.4 Varieties of Annuity Products

The annuity market offers a range of products to fit different financial perspectives and risk appetites. Fixed, Indexed, and Variable Annuities provide options from guaranteed returns to market-linked growth, addressing varying investor needs and preferences. Market Value Adjusted Annuities add another layer of choice, blending fixed returns with market participation. This spectrum of annuity products enables individuals to select the type that best aligns with their financial goals, market outlook, and risk tolerance, facilitating customized retirement planning solutions.

6.5 Practical Applications of Annuities

Annuities serve multiple financial purposes beyond just providing retirement income. From supporting estate planning to funding educational expenses, the versatility of annuities makes them a valuable tool in a wide range of financial strategies. Their ability to offer tax-deferred growth and integrate into various retirement and savings plans, such as IRAs, enhances their appeal in comprehensive financial planning. Whether used for immediate income needs or long-term growth, annuities can be structured to meet diverse financial objectives, making them a fundamental component of personal finance and retirement planning.

6.6 Annuity Suitability

Selecting the appropriate annuity is a critical decision that requires careful consideration of personal financial circumstances, goals, and risk tolerance. Suitability assessment ensures that the chosen annuity aligns with the individual's broader financial strategy and retirement objectives. Factors such as financial needs, tax implications, and estate planning goals must be evaluated to determine the most appropriate annuity product. This careful alignment ensures that individuals can maximize the benefits of their annuity, securing their financial future while meeting current needs and long-term objectives.

Case Study: Strategic Retirement Planning with Annuities

Background:

John Doe, a 60-year-old soon-to-be retiree, is evaluating his retirement options. With a significant pension pot and personal savings, John is exploring how to best manage his assets to provide a stable income throughout retirement.

Scenario:

John wants to ensure a steady income stream that keeps pace with inflation and allows for unexpected expenses. He is considering investing a portion of his savings into an annuity product.

Policy Details:

After consulting with a financial advisor, John decides on a Deferred Variable Annuity with an inflation-adjusted rider. This annuity will allow his capital to grow until he decides to start receiving payments and will adjust the payouts according to inflation rates.

Action Taken:

John allocates $200,000 from his retirement fund into the chosen annuity product, with a plan to start receiving payments in five years, aligning with his retirement date.

Outcome:

By the time John retires, his annuity has grown significantly, providing him with a higher initial income than initially projected. The inflation-adjustment feature ensures his purchasing power is maintained.

Conclusion:

John's decision to invest in a Deferred Variable Annuity with an inflation-adjusted rider effectively secures a portion of his retirement income, providing peace of mind and financial stability.

Discussion Points for Insurance Exam Preparation:

- The importance of understanding different annuity types and their respective benefits.
- Evaluating client needs to determine the most suitable annuity product.
- The impact of inflation on retirement savings and how certain annuities can address this issue.

Frequently Asked Questions:

1. What is the difference between Immediate and Deferred Annuities?

Immediate Annuities start paying out shortly after the initial investment, while Deferred Annuities allow the investment to grow before starting the payout phase.

2. Can you explain what a Variable Annuity is?

A Variable Annuity allows the owner to invest in various investment options, such as stocks and bonds, with payouts that depend on the performance of these investments.

3. What are the tax implications of investing in an annuity?

Annuities offer tax-deferred growth, meaning taxes on earnings are not paid until withdrawals are made.

4. How does an inflation-adjusted rider work in an annuity?

This rider increases your annuity payments annually to keep pace with inflation, thereby maintaining your purchasing power over time.

5. What is annuity suitability, and why is it important?

Annuity suitability ensures that the chosen annuity product aligns with the individual's financial situation, goals, and risk tolerance, ensuring they receive the most appropriate product for their needs.

6. What should I consider when choosing between a Fixed and a Variable Annuity?

Consider your risk tolerance, financial goals, and the need for predictable income. Fixed Annuities offer guaranteed returns, while Variable Annuities provide potential for higher returns but come with greater risk.

Chapter 7: Federal Tax Implications for Life Insurance and Annuities

7.1 Overview of Tax Considerations

Understanding the intricate tax implications associated with life insurance and annuities is essential for comprehensive financial planning. These implications influence decisions related to the purchase, maintenance, and eventual payout of these financial products. A well-informed approach ensures individuals can maximize benefits while minimizing tax liabilities. Federal tax laws have significant bearings on the way life insurance and annuity proceeds are handled, taxed, and transferred. This section aims to demystify the complex interplay between these financial instruments and federal tax regulations, providing a solid foundation for making informed decisions that align with long-term financial goals.

7.2 Tax Aspects of Personal Life Insurance

Life insurance is not only a tool for providing financial security but also a product with distinct tax characteristics. Policyowners should understand the nuances of how life insurance is treated under tax law, including the taxation of cash value accumulations and policy dividends. The implications of policy loans and the act of surrendering a policy are equally important, as they can lead to taxable events. Moreover, the manner in which life insurance proceeds are taxed upon being passed to beneficiaries can significantly affect estate planning and the overall tax burden on the estate. This segment explores these elements in depth, clarifying common misconceptions and outlining strategies for leveraging life insurance within a tax-efficient framework.

7.3 Modified Endowment Contracts (MECs)

Modified Endowment Contracts hold a unique place within life insurance taxation. Classified differently due to the application of the Seven-Pay Test, MECs attract different tax rules compared to standard life insurance policies. Policyholders must be cognizant of the implications associated with MECs, particularly regarding the taxation of policy withdrawals and loans. This section delves into the criteria that define MECs, the tax ramifications of exceeding the Seven-Pay threshold, and the strategies for managing MECs to avoid adverse tax consequences.

7.4 Taxation of Non-Qualified Annuities

Non-qualified annuities present distinct tax considerations during both the accumulation and distribution phases. The tax treatment of these annuities is contingent upon several factors, including the annuity's ownership structure and the timing of withdrawals. This discussion extends to the concept of the exclusion ratio and its impact on determining the taxable portion of annuity payments. Special attention is given to the differential treatment of individually-owned versus corporate-owned annuities, highlighting tax implications particularly relevant in estate planning and succession scenarios.

7.5 IRA Tax Considerations

Individual Retirement Accounts (IRAs), both Traditional and Roth, offer unique tax benefits and implications. This section provides an in-depth look at the tax treatment of contributions, accumulation, and distributions associated with these retirement vehicles. It covers critical considerations such as the tax deductibility of contributions, the tax-free growth of Roth IRAs, and the penalties and tax consequences associated with early withdrawals. Additionally, the estate planning implications of IRAs, including the handling of inherited IRAs and the application of required minimum distributions, are thoroughly examined.

7.6 Rollovers and Transfers

Successfully navigating the rules governing rollovers and transfers between retirement accounts is vital to maintaining their tax-advantaged status. This part of the chapter outlines the specific conditions under which individuals can execute rollovers between different types of retirement accounts without incurring immediate tax liabilities. It also covers the nuances of direct versus indirect rollovers, the timing rules, and the potential tax consequences of failing to adhere to IRS guidelines.

7.7 Section 1035 Exchanges

Section 1035 of the Internal Revenue Code allows for the tax-free exchange of certain types of insurance policies and annuities. This provision offers policyholders the flexibility to adapt their financial planning strategies without incurring immediate tax liabilities. This segment explores the eligibility criteria for these exchanges, the types of contracts that qualify, and practical considerations to ensure compliance and optimize financial outcomes.

Chapter 8: Understanding Qualified Plans

8.1 Overview of Qualified Plans

Qualified plans form a critical component of financial security, offering structured methods for individuals and employees to save for retirement while benefiting from substantial tax advantages. These plans are designed to encourage long-term savings and provide financial stability into retirement, with specific rules and benefits as defined by the Internal Revenue Service (IRS) and the Employee Retirement Income Security Act (ERISA). Understanding these plans is essential for effective retirement planning and ensuring compliance with federal laws to maximize tax benefits.

8.2 Key Requirements for Qualified Plans

Qualified plans must adhere to stringent regulatory standards and prerequisites set forth by federal guidelines to qualify for tax advantages. These requirements include nondiscrimination rules to ensure benefits are not heavily skewed in favor of high earners, minimum coverage standards, contribution limits, and rules regarding distributions and loans. Compliance with these standards is critical for the plan's qualification status and its ability to provide tax-deferred growth and contributions.

8.3 Tax Implications for Qualified Plans

The tax benefits associated with qualified plans are significant, providing incentives for both employers and employees to contribute to retirement savings. Contributions to these plans are typically tax-deductible, reducing taxable income for the year they are made. Investment growth within these plans accumulates tax-deferred until withdrawals begin, typically in retirement when the individual may be in a lower tax bracket. However, specific rules apply to distributions, including penalties for early withdrawal and requirements for minimum distributions starting at a certain age, impacting the tax situation for plan participants.

8.4 Types and Features of Qualified Plans

There is a variety of qualified plans available, each designed to meet the different needs of employers and employees. Simplified Employee Pensions (SEPs) allow employers to make contributions to traditional IRAs set up for employees, ideal for small businesses and self-employed individuals. Profit-sharing plans enable employees to share in the profits of the company. 401(k) plans are perhaps the most well-known, allowing employees to contribute a portion of their wages to individual accounts. SIMPLE plans and 403(b) Tax-Sheltered Annuities offer additional retirement savings options, particularly suitable for small businesses and non-profit organizations, respectively. Each plan type has unique features, benefits, and rules, making it crucial to understand the differences to select the most appropriate plan for individual and business needs.

Case Study: Maximizing Retirement Savings through Qualified Plans

Background:

Susan, a 45-year-old small business owner, seeks to establish a retirement savings plan for herself and her five employees to enhance financial security and take advantage of tax benefits.

Scenario:

Susan's business has been steadily growing, and she wishes to provide retirement benefits to attract and retain quality employees while also securing her own financial future.

Policy Details:

After consulting with a financial advisor, Susan is considering setting up a Simplified Employee Pension (SEP) plan due to its ease of administration and flexible contribution options.

Action Taken:

Susan implemented the SEP plan, allowing for employer contributions to traditional IRAs established in each employee's name. She decided to contribute 6% of each employee's annual salary to the SEP plan.

Outcome:

All employees, including Susan, appreciated the added benefit, leading to increased job satisfaction and loyalty. The contributions reduced the taxable income for Susan's business, leading to tax savings, while providing a solid foundation for retirement savings for all involved.

Conclusion:

By understanding and utilizing qualified plans, Susan was able to provide valuable retirement benefits to her employees and herself, resulting in tax savings for her business and enhancing employee satisfaction and retention.

Discussion Points for Insurance Exam Preparation:

- The importance of choosing the right type of qualified plan for different business sizes and structures.

- Understanding the tax implications and benefits of employer contributions to retirement plans.

- Compliance requirements for qualified plans under ERISA and IRS regulations.

Frequently Asked Questions:

1. What distinguishes a qualified plan from other retirement savings options?

Qualified plans meet specific IRS and ERISA guidelines, offering tax advantages such as tax-deferred growth and deductible contributions.

2. How does a Simplified Employee Pension (SEP) plan work?

A SEP plan allows employers to contribute directly to traditional IRAs established for their employees, with contributions being tax-deductible for the employer and tax-deferred for the employees until withdrawal.

3. What are the main benefits of a 401(k) plan for employees?

Employees can contribute a portion of their salary on a pre-tax basis to a 401(k) plan, reducing their taxable income and allowing their savings to grow tax-deferred until retirement.

4. Can self-employed individuals establish qualified plans?

Yes, self-employed individuals can establish SEP, SIMPLE, and individual 401(k) plans to save for retirement while enjoying tax benefits.

5. What are required minimum distributions (RMDs), and when do they begin?

RMDs are mandatory annual withdrawals that must start from qualified plans and IRAs by April 1st of the year following the year in which the account holder turns 72 (or 70½ if born before July 1, 1949).

6. What are the consequences of early withdrawals from qualified plans?

Early withdrawals, generally taken before age 59½, may be subject to a 10% penalty in addition to being taxed as ordinary income.

Chapter 9: Fundamentals of Health Insurance

9.1 Introduction to Health Insurance

Health insurance stands as a fundamental element in managing individual and family health care costs. It serves as a financial safeguard against expenses arising from unforeseen medical events such as accidents or illnesses. The significance of understanding different perils like accidental injuries and sickness cannot be overstated, as this knowledge forms the basis for selecting the appropriate health insurance coverage that aligns with personal or family needs, ensuring that medical care is accessible without overwhelming financial strain.

9.2 Understanding Health Insurance Perils

In the realm of health coverage, perils refer to the specific events or conditions that trigger the need for medical attention and subsequent financial coverage. These typically encompass accidental injuries, which are unexpected and unintentional physical harms, and sickness, which includes any illness or disease requiring medical treatment. The clear distinction and understanding of these perils are essential, as they directly influence the type of health insurance coverage one might choose. For instance, some policies may offer more comprehensive coverage for chronic diseases, while others may focus on emergency accidental injuries.

9.3 Types of Losses and Benefits

Health insurance is designed to cover various types of losses, each contributing to the financial security and well-being of the insured. The primary categories include:

- Disability: This covers a portion of the income lost due to the inability to work because of an injury or illness.

- Medical: This broad category covers expenses from routine doctor visits to complex surgical procedures, hospital stays, and emergency medical care.

- Dental: Dental coverage typically includes preventive services like cleanings and check-ups, as well as procedures such as fillings, crowns, and root canals.

- Long-term Care: This type of insurance covers services not typically covered by regular health insurance or Medicare, such as assistance with daily living activities for those with a chronic illness or disability.

9.4 Health Insurance Policy Categories

- Health insurance policies can be broadly categorized to help individuals make informed decisions based on their specific needs:

- Individual policies cater to single persons and offer varying levels of coverage based on chosen plans and premiums.

- Group policies are generally provided by employers or organizations, offering benefits to employees or members as part of a collective agreement.

- Private versus government coverage distinguishes between policies offered by private insurance companies and those provided through government programs like Medicare and Medicaid.

Limited versus comprehensive policies differ in scope, where limited policies might only cover specific diseases or events, whereas comprehensive policies provide broader coverage.

9.5 Overview of Limited Health Policies

Limited health policies are specialized insurance plans designed to cover specific perils or offer limited amounts of coverage. These can include:

- Accident-only policies that provide coverage exclusively for injuries resulting from accidents, excluding illnesses.

- Specified disease policies designed to cover the costs associated with treating specific diseases such as cancer or heart disease.

- Hospital indemnity policies that offer a fixed cash benefit during hospital stays, which can help cover incidental costs.

- Credit disability insurance, which is intended to cover loan payments for individuals unable to work due to injury or illness.

9.6 Common Health Insurance Exclusions

Health insurance policies often exclude certain conditions or types of treatments from coverage. Typical exclusions might include pre-existing conditions, cosmetic surgery, and experimental treatments. Understanding these exclusions is crucial to avoid unexpected out-of-pocket expenses and to ensure that one's health insurance plan aligns with their health care needs.

9.7 Responsibilities of Health Insurance Producers

Health insurance producers, including agents and brokers, play a pivotal role in the health insurance market. They are responsible for adhering to strict marketing requirements, providing clear and accurate information during sales presentations, and ensuring that potential policyholders understand the coverage options available to them. They must also adhere to regulations regarding disclosure and avoid common errors or omissions that could mislead consumers.

9.8 Individual Health Insurance Underwriting

The underwriting process in individual health insurance involves evaluating an applicant's medical history, lifestyle, and other risk factors to determine coverage eligibility and premium rates. This process can include medical examinations and the review of medical records. Legal considerations, such as regulations against unfair discrimination, guide this process to ensure fair treatment for all applicants.

9.9 Health Insurance Replacement Considerations

When considering replacing health insurance, it is important to weigh the new policy's benefits, limitations, and exclusions against the current coverage. Understanding the underwriting requirements and potential implications for existing conditions is essential. Additionally, considering the liability for errors and omissions can help in making an informed decision.

9.10 Mandated Provisions in Health Insurance

State-mandated provisions in health insurance policies can vary significantly, impacting coverage and consumer rights. These provisions often include required benefits, appeal processes for denied claims, and rules regarding policy renewals. Familiarity with these provisions is crucial for both policyholders and those within the insurance industry to ensure compliance and to understand the protections afforded under the law.

Remember, you can find practice exam questions related to "Fundamentals of Health Insurance" at the end of the book to aid in your exam preparation and understanding of this chapter's content

Frequently Asked Questions for Insurance Professionals

1. How do I determine the appropriate level of coverage for a client?

Evaluate the client's financial situation, health status, family medical history, and future needs. Consider factors such as income, dependents, existing debts, and savings. Use these assessments to guide clients towards plans that offer adequate protection without overextending their budget.

2. What strategies can be employed to handle clients with pre-existing conditions?

Educate clients about the provisions of the Affordable Care Act concerning pre-existing conditions. Discuss the importance of continuous coverage and explore state-specific programs or high-risk pools as alternatives. Guide clients through the underwriting process and help them understand their rights and options.

3. How do changes in legislation affect health insurance policies and coverage options?

Stay informed about current and upcoming health insurance legislation and regulatory changes. Understand how new laws such as modifications to the Affordable Care Act or state-specific health mandates impact policy offerings, premiums, and benefits. Communicate these changes effectively to clients and provide guidance on how to adapt their coverage accordingly.

4. What is the best approach for explaining deductibles, co-payments, and coinsurance to clients?

Use clear, straightforward language and real-life examples to explain how deductibles, co-payments, and coinsurance work. Create scenarios that demonstrate how these costs are applied in different medical situations. Offer to review their current health expenses to illustrate potential out-of-pocket costs under different plans.

5. How should I advise clients on choosing between different health insurance policy categories?

Discuss the client's healthcare needs, preferences, and budget. Compare the features, benefits, and limitations of individual vs. group policies, private vs. government coverage, and limited vs. comprehensive policies. Highlight the trade-offs between broader coverage and higher premiums versus lower costs and restricted benefits.

6. What are common errors or omissions in health insurance sales, and how can they be avoided?

Common errors include inadequate needs assessment, misrepresentations of policy terms, and failing to provide all legally required disclosures. Avoid these by conducting thorough client interviews, continuously educating yourself about policy details, and adhering strictly to ethical and legal standards.

7. How do I navigate the underwriting process for individual health insurance with clients?

Explain the underwriting process clearly, including the types of information needed, such as medical history and financial data. Prepare clients for possible medical exams or requests for additional information. Discuss how different risk factors might affect their premiums and coverage options.

8. What are the key considerations when advising clients on health insurance replacement?

Review the benefits, limitations, and exclusions of both the old and new policies. Ensure clients understand potential gaps in coverage, changes in premiums, and the implications of pre-existing condition clauses. Advise on the timing of the switch to avoid lapses in coverage.

9. How can I ensure compliance with state-mandated health insurance provisions?

Keep updated with state-specific insurance laws and regulations. Attend continuing education courses and seminars. Regularly review your state's insurance department resources and guidelines. Apply this knowledge when advising clients and ensure all policy recommendations meet or exceed these mandates.

Chapter 10: Key Provisions in Individual Health Insurance Policies

10.1 Overview of Individual Health Insurance Policy Provisions

Individual health insurance policies are essential tools for managing personal health and financial risks. These policies come with a set of standard provisions designed to protect the rights and outline the responsibilities of both the policyholder and the insurance company. Understanding these provisions is critical for anyone holding or considering an individual health insurance policy. They dictate the terms of coverage, claim procedures, premium payments, and other key aspects of the insurance agreement.

The importance of these provisions cannot be overstated. They form the legal foundation of the insurance contract, setting forth the promises of the insurer and the expectations for the insured. For policyholders, a thorough understanding of these terms is essential for effective policy management. It enables informed decision-making and helps ensure that individuals can maximize the benefits of their coverage while minimizing out-of-pocket expenses.

10.2 Mandatory Policy Provisions

Mandatory policy provisions are those terms and conditions that, by law, must be included in all individual health insurance policies. These provisions are designed to ensure fairness and transparency in the insurance process and provide protections for both the insured and the insurer. They include the entire contract clause, which mandates that the insurance policy and any endorsements or riders form the complete agreement between the insured and the insurer.

One of the key mandatory provisions is the time limit on certain defenses. This sets a timeframe during which the insurer can dispute claims based on misstatements in the application. Another critical provision is the grace period, typically 30 days, which allows policyholders to make a late payment without losing coverage. The reinstatement provision outlines the conditions under which a lapsed policy can be reactivated.

Understanding these mandatory provisions is crucial for policyholders. They provide a safety net, ensuring that individuals have time to rectify mistakes and maintain coverage even in challenging circumstances. Additionally, they establish the legal ground rules for the insurance agreement, ensuring that policyholders know what to expect and what is expected of them.

10.3 Additional Contractual Provisions

Beyond the mandatory elements, individual health insurance policies often include additional contractual provisions tailored to the specific details of the coverage. These can include clauses addressing changes in occupation, which might affect the risk profile of the insured, and misstatements of age, which can impact premium calculations and benefits.

Another important aspect covered under additional provisions is the coordination of benefits. This outlines how the policy will interact with other forms of health insurance, ensuring that benefits from multiple sources are coordinated efficiently to cover medical expenses without overcompensation.

These additional provisions are vital for creating a comprehensive and effective insurance plan. They allow policies to be personalized to the individual's needs and circumstances, providing flexibility and ensuring that coverage is both appropriate and cost-effective. For policyholders, understanding these provisions is key to managing their health insurance effectively and avoiding unexpected financial burdens.

10.4 Special Policy Provisions

Special policy provisions offer additional benefits and options to policyholders, enhancing the flexibility and value of the health insurance policy. For instance, the free look period is a common provision that allows new policyholders a specified period, typically 10 to 30 days, to review the policy and return it for a full refund if not satisfied.

The insuring clause and consideration clause are fundamental components that define the scope of coverage and the premium payment obligations, respectively. These clauses lay the foundation for the insurance agreement, establishing what the insurer agrees to cover and what the policyholder agrees to pay.

Renewability clauses are particularly significant, defining the terms under which a policy may be continued or terminated. These range from noncancelable, where the policy cannot be canceled by the insurer as long as premiums are paid, to policies that are renewable at the insurer's discretion.

Understanding these special provisions is crucial for policyholders, as they significantly affect the policy's long-term viability and the insured's financial security. They provide critical information on how the policy can adapt to changing life circumstances, such as entering active military service, and outline the insured's rights and options for maintaining coverage.

10.5 Understanding Renewability and Cancellation Clauses

Renewability and cancellation clauses are among the most important aspects of individual health insurance policies. They dictate the circumstances under which a policy may be renewed or canceled, directly impacting the insured's long-term health coverage and financial security.

Policies with a noncancelable clause offer the greatest security, guaranteeing renewal as long as premiums are paid. On the other hand, policies that allow cancellation at the insurer's discretion provide less stability and can lead to increased uncertainty for the policyholder.

Understanding the specifics of these clauses is essential for anyone with or considering individual health insurance. They directly affect the insured's ability to maintain continuous coverage and manage their health care costs effectively. By fully understanding these terms, policyholders can make informed decisions about their insurance, ensuring that they have the coverage they need when they need it.

In conclusion, individual health insurance policies are complex documents with various provisions that can significantly impact the insured's health care and financial well-being. Understanding these provisions is essential for effective policy management and ensuring that individuals can navigate the complexities of their coverage. By becoming familiar with the key elements of these policies, from mandatory and additional contractual provisions to special and renewability clauses, policyholders can make informed decisions, reduce their financial risks, and secure the best possible health outcomes for themselves and their families.

The knowledge of how individual health insurance works, the rights and responsibilities it entails, and the strategies for managing it effectively is not just beneficial, but indispensable for anyone looking to safeguard their health and financial future. As health care needs and the legal landscape continue to evolve, staying informed and proactive about health insurance coverage becomes increasingly crucial.

Remember, the goal of this guide is not only to help you pass your state life insurance and health insurance exams but also to equip you with the knowledge to make wise insurance decisions throughout your life. By understanding the intricacies of individual health insurance policies, you can ensure that you and your loved ones are adequately protected, no matter what the future holds.

Case Study: Navigating Health Insurance for a Growing Family

Background:

The Johnson family, consisting of John, his wife Linda, and their two children, have been covered under John's individual health insurance plan. With the arrival of their third child expected in a few months, they realize the need to reassess their health insurance coverage to ensure it meets the growing family's needs.

Scenario:

The Johnsons are concerned about the increasing healthcare expenses and whether their current health insurance plan will adequately cover the costs associated with prenatal care, childbirth, and pediatric care for their newborn, in addition to ongoing medical needs for the entire family.

Policy Details:

John's current policy is a high-deductible health plan (HDHP) with a Health Savings Account (HSA), primarily covering him and offering partial benefits for his family. It includes standard provisions but lacks comprehensive maternity and pediatric coverage.

Action Taken:

The Johnsons consult with an insurance advisor to explore their options. They consider switching to a family health insurance plan with lower deductibles, better maternity care, and expanded pediatric coverage. They also explore adding a maternity rider and increasing the policy's scope to cover preventive and routine pediatric care.

Outcome:

After reviewing several plans, the Johnsons opt for a more comprehensive family health insurance policy that covers prenatal, maternity, and pediatric care. They transition before the birth of their third child, ensuring full coverage for Linda's pregnancy and the newborn's medical needs.

Conclusion:

By proactively reassessing their health insurance coverage and making necessary adjustments, the Johnson family secures a policy that better suits their evolving needs, ensuring peace of mind and financial stability as they welcome their new member.

Discussion Points for Insurance Exam Preparation:

- Importance of understanding policy provisions and their impact on coverage.

- Strategies for adjusting health insurance coverage in response to life changes.

- Evaluating the benefits and drawbacks of different types of health insurance plans for family coverage.

Frequently Asked Questions:

1. What should I consider when choosing an individual health insurance plan?

Evaluate your and your family's health needs, consider the coverage for preventive services, check the network of doctors and hospitals, understand the costs including premiums, deductibles, and out-of-pocket limits.

2. How do mandatory policy provisions affect my health insurance?

Mandatory provisions ensure your policy adheres to state laws and regulations, providing basic rights and protections, such as the right to appeal a denied claim and ensuring a grace period for late payments.

3. What are additional contractual provisions in health insurance?

These are terms and conditions added to your policy beyond the standard mandatory provisions, which might include specific coverage limits, additional benefits, or clauses tailored to individual policies.

4. Why are special policy provisions important in health insurance?

Special provisions, such as pre-existing condition exclusions or maternity benefits, can significantly impact the scope and utility of your coverage, affecting how and when you receive benefits.

5. Can I change my health insurance policy provisions?

While some provisions are mandated by law and cannot be changed, others may be adjusted based on your insurance company's policies and your specific health insurance plan.

6. What is the importance of renewability and cancellation clauses in health insurance policies?

These clauses determine under what conditions your policy can be renewed or canceled, impacting your long-term coverage and financial security. Understanding these can help you choose a plan that provides stability and meets your long-term health care needs.

Chapter 11: Disability Income and Related Insurance

11.1 Introduction to Disability Income Insurance

Disability income insurance stands as a cornerstone in individual financial security strategies, designed to provide income in the event that an individual is unable to work due to illness or injury. This type of insurance is crucial because it not only offers financial protection but also ensures that the policyholder can maintain their standard of living during periods of non-employment due to health issues. Understanding the various policy provisions, benefits, and the different types of disability income insurance available is vital for anyone seeking to safeguard their future earnings and financial stability.

11.2 Eligibility for Disability Benefits

Eligibility for disability benefits under a disability income insurance policy typically hinges on the policy's definition of disability, which may vary between 'own occupation'—where benefits are paid if the insured cannot perform the duties of their specific occupation—and 'any occupation'—where benefits are only paid if the insured cannot perform the duties of any occupation for which they are reasonably suited by education, training, or experience. Additionally, conditions such as presumptive disability, where certain medical conditions automatically qualify one for benefits, and the requirement for ongoing physician care to confirm the disability, play a crucial role in eligibility determination.

11.3 Features of Individual Disability Income Insurance

Individual disability income insurance policies provide a range of features designed to meet the diverse needs of policyholders. These features typically include basic total disability plans, which define how and when benefits are paid, and the structure of those benefits. The policy details will often outline specific elimination and benefit periods as well as the conditions under which a waiver of premium may apply. Additionally, the coordination of these disability benefits with other types of benefits, such as social insurance or workers' compensation, is crucial. The distinction between occupational vs. nonoccupational coverage, as well as partial vs. residual benefits, must be clearly understood. Policyholders should also be aware of how policy provisions like Cost of Living Adjustments (COLA) and Future Increase Options (FIO) riders can impact their benefits.

11.4 Underwriting of Individual Disability Insurance

The underwriting process for individual disability insurance takes into account various factors, including the applicant's occupation, income level, and health status. Insurers assess these factors to determine the risk of insuring the individual and to establish premium rates. The relationship between the insured's earnings and their insurance coverage is critical, as it affects the amount of benefit the policyholder is eligible to receive in the event of a disability.

11.5 Overview of Group Disability Income Insurance

Group disability income insurance typically offers coverage to employees as part of an employer-sponsored benefits package. These plans can be categorized into short-term and long-term disability plans, each with different coverage terms, benefit periods, and eligibility requirements. Understanding the distinctions between these types of plans is essential for both employers offering the benefits and employees receiving them.

11.6 Business Disability Insurance Concepts

In the context of business, disability insurance can play a pivotal role. Key person disability insurance protects a company financially in the event that a crucial employee becomes disabled. Similarly, disability buy-sell insurance provides a mechanism for business continuation if an owner or significant stakeholder becomes disabled.

11.7 Understanding Social Security Disability

Social Security disability benefits are available to individuals who meet the federal criteria for disability, typically involving a rigorous application process and specific medical criteria. Understanding the definition of disability according to Social Security standards and the associated waiting periods is essential for advising clients on their eligibility and potential benefits.

11.8 Workers' Compensation and Disability

Workers' compensation provides benefits to employees who are injured or become ill as a direct result of their job. Eligibility for these benefits, as well as the relationship between workers' compensation and other disability income sources, is an important area of understanding for professionals in the insurance industry.

Case Study: John's Journey Through Disability Coverage

Background:

John, a 40-year-old software developer, recently purchased an individual disability income insurance policy after realizing the financial risks associated with long-term absence from work due to illness or injury. Despite being in good health, John recognized the importance of securing his income, especially since he is the primary breadwinner for his family.

Scenario:

Six months after acquiring the policy, John was involved in a serious car accident resulting in a complex leg fracture that rendered him unable to work. Following the accident, John was hospitalized for two weeks and then required extensive home recovery and physical therapy.

Policy Details:

John's disability income insurance policy includes a 90-day elimination period, meaning he must be disabled for 90 days before receiving benefit payments. The policy covers 60% of his monthly income and includes a waiver of premium feature. It is an "own occupation" policy, meaning John is considered disabled if he cannot perform the duties of his specific occupation as a software developer.

Action Taken:

After the accident, John filed a claim with his insurance company, providing all necessary medical documentation and proof of income. The insurer evaluated his claim, confirming the disability as per the policy's terms. After the 90-day elimination period, John began receiving monthly benefit payments, allowing him to focus on recovery without the stress of lost income.

Outcome:

John spent four months in recovery before he could return to work part-time. During this period, his disability income insurance continued to provide partial benefits to supplement his reduced income, thanks to the policy's partial disability feature. Once John resumed full-time work, the benefits ceased, but the financial support during his recovery was crucial in maintaining his family's standard of living and covering medical expenses.

Conclusion:

This case study underscores the importance of understanding the features and provisions of disability income insurance. It highlights the critical role such insurance can play in financial stability during unexpected health crises. Remember, while each policy and situation is unique, having the right coverage can provide essential support during challenging times.

Discussion Points for Insurance Exam Preparation:

- The importance of the elimination period and its impact on claim timing.
- The difference between "own occupation" and "any occupation" definitions of disability.
- How partial disability benefits can provide support during a gradual return to work.
- The role of waiver of premium features in maintaining policy benefits without the burden of continued premium payments during disability.

Frequently Asked Questions

1. How does the elimination period in a disability insurance policy work?

The elimination period is the time between the onset of a disability and when benefit payments begin. It functions like a deductible, with policyholders choosing the length of this period based on their financial capability and needs.

2. Can a policyholder work in a different occupation while receiving disability benefits?

This depends on the policy's definition of disability. If the policy specifies 'own occupation,' the policyholder may receive benefits while working in a different field. Under 'any occupation' policies, this may not be possible.

3. What is the typical duration for long-term disability benefits?

Long-term disability benefits can vary but often last until the policyholder recovers, reaches a specific age, such as 65 or 67, or for a set period such as 2, 5, or 10 years.

4. How do I adjust coverage as my income increases?

Policies with Future Increase Options (FIO) allow policyholders to increase coverage as their income grows, typically without additional medical underwriting.

Chapter 12: Overview of Medical Plans

12.1 Introduction to Medical Plans

Health insurance is a critical component in managing personal health care and financial well-being. It mitigates the financial risk associated with high medical costs due to illnesses, accidents, or other health issues. Understanding the foundational concepts of health insurance, including the types of medical plans available, is crucial. This understanding aids in making informed decisions about health coverage, ensuring that individuals are adequately protected against various health perils such as accidental injuries and sickness.

12.2 Understanding Health Insurance Perils

In health coverage, perils refer to the specific risks or conditions covered, including accidental injuries and sickness. These perils form the basis of claims and determine the scope of coverage. Accidental injury coverage typically includes events that are sudden and unforeseen, while sickness coverage pertains to health conditions that arise during the policy period. Understanding these definitions is essential for policyholders to know what is covered and under what circumstances, facilitating better utilization of their health insurance benefits.

12.3 Types of Losses and Benefits

Health insurance policies are designed to cover various types of losses, including:

- Disability: Provides income replacement in case of inability to work due to illness or injury.

- Medical: Covers costs associated with medical treatment, surgeries, and hospital stays.

- Dental: Addresses expenses related to dental care, including routine checkups, cleanings, and dental procedures.

- Long-term Care: Offers coverage for services like home care, nursing home, or assisted living for individuals unable to perform basic living activities.

The benefits provided under these categories ensure financial protection against the high costs associated with different health-related losses. Understanding each type of loss and the corresponding benefits is vital for selecting the right health insurance coverage.

12.4 Health Insurance Policy Categories

Health insurance policies can be broadly categorized into individual and group policies, with distinctions also made between private and government coverage. Individual policies are purchased by individuals, offering personalized coverage but typically at higher costs. Group policies are offered by employers or organizations, providing coverage to a group of people under one contract, usually at a reduced cost per person. Government coverage includes programs like Medicare and Medicaid, designed for specific populations. Understanding these categories helps individuals choose the most suitable insurance based on their needs and circumstances.

12.5 Overview of Limited Health Policies

Limited health policies offer coverage for specific perils or set amounts, which might include:

- Accident-only: Coverage solely for accidents, excluding sickness.

- Specified Disease: Provides benefits for a designated disease or illness.

- Hospital Indemnity: Offers a fixed amount per day of hospitalization.

- Credit Disability: Makes loan payments if the insured becomes disabled.

- Blanket Insurance: Covers groups of people for specific activities or events.

Understanding the limitations and specific coverage of these policies is crucial for consumers to avoid unexpected gaps in their health coverage.

12.6 Common Health Insurance Exclusions

Health insurance policies typically exclude certain conditions, treatments, or activities from coverage. Common exclusions may include pre-existing conditions, elective surgeries, cosmetic procedures, and injuries from high-risk activities. Being aware of these exclusions is important for policyholders to understand the limits of their coverage and avoid denied claims.

12.7 Responsibilities of Health Insurance Producers

Health insurance producers, whether agents or brokers, play a crucial role in the insurance marketplace. They are responsible for:

- Understanding and communicating key marketing requirements and advertising regulations.

- Ensuring that clients are informed about their coverage options and the details of their policies.

- Adhering to ethical standards during sales presentations and providing an accurate outline of coverage.

- Being aware of disclosure requirements and avoiding common errors or omissions that could mislead potential policyholders.

12.8 Individual Health Insurance Underwriting

The underwriting process for individual health insurance involves assessing the risk presented by the applicant based on factors such as medical history, age, and lifestyle. Underwriters use this information to determine eligibility, coverage terms, and premiums. The process is governed by laws and regulations that prevent unfair discrimination and ensure that risk classification is based on sound underwriting principles.

12.9 Health Insurance Replacement Considerations

When considering replacing health insurance, individuals should evaluate the new policy's benefits, limitations, and exclusions compared to their current coverage. They should also understand the underwriting requirements and potential impacts on their premiums and benefits. Additionally, understanding the liability producers hold for errors and omissions during the replacement process can guide individuals in making informed decisions.

12.10 Mandated Provisions in Health Insurance

State laws often mandate specific provisions that must be included in health insurance policies, affecting coverage and consumer rights. These mandates can include coverage for certain conditions, treatments, and populations. Understanding these mandates is crucial for policyholders and professionals in the insurance industry to ensure compliance and adequate coverage.

Frequently Asked Questions:

1. How do fee-for-service and prepaid medical plans differ?

Fee-for-service plans typically allow more freedom in choosing healthcare providers and are based on the reimbursement of covered services. Prepaid plans, like HMOs, offer a range of services for a set fee and often require the use of network providers.

2. What is the difference between a PPO and an HMO?

PPOs provide more flexibility in selecting healthcare providers and often cover a portion of out-of-network care costs. HMOs generally require members to select a primary care physician and get referrals for specialist services, focusing on preventive care within a network of providers.

3. What are common limitations in major medical insurance?

Common limitations can include annual and lifetime coverage caps, restricted coverage for certain procedures or conditions, and waiting periods for specific benefits.

4. How does the Affordable Care Act affect individual health plans?

The ACA introduced reforms such as prohibiting denial of coverage based on pre-existing conditions, extending coverage for young adults on parental plans, and establishing health insurance marketplaces for individual plan shopping.

Case Study: Managing Chronic Conditions under New Health Plan

Background:

John, a 50-year-old with type 2 diabetes, is evaluating new health insurance options.

Scenario:

John is considering switching from a traditional fee-for-service plan to a managed care plan to save on monthly premiums.

Policy Details:

The new plan is a high-deductible health plan (HDHP) with a health savings account (HSA), offering lower premiums but higher out-of-pocket costs.

Action Taken:

John reviewed the new plan's coverage for chronic conditions and compared it to his current plan's benefits, especially regarding diabetes management.

Outcome:

John decided that while the HDHP offered savings on premiums, it required more out-of-pocket spending for his diabetes care. He opted to stay with his current plan but also explored additional cost-saving measures.

Conclusion:

Careful comparison of health plans is essential, especially for individuals managing chronic conditions.

Discussion Points for Insurance Exam Preparation:

- Compare and contrast the coverage for chronic conditions under different health plans.

- Assess the financial implications of switching from a fee-for-service to a managed care plan.

- Explore the benefits and limitations of using an HSA with a high-deductible plan for managing health expenses.

Chapter 13: Essentials of Group Health Insurance

13.1 Introduction to Group Health Insurance

Group health insurance is a cornerstone in the landscape of employee benefits, providing members with essential health coverage under a collective policy. This insurance framework contrasts with individual health plans by offering standardized coverage to a group, leading to generally lower costs per member due to the larger risk pool. Key to understanding group insurance is recognizing the nuances between group contracts, which the employer or organizing entity holds, and individual certificates of coverage, which detail the specific protections available to each plan member.

13.2 Features of Group Insurance

Distinctive attributes of group health insurance include:

Community Rating vs. Experience Rating: Premiums may be set based on the collective health data of the group (experience rating) or spread across a wider community, disregarding individual group data (community rating).

Master Policy and Certificates of Coverage: The group holds a master policy, while members receive certificates outlining individual coverage details.

13.3 Eligible Groups for Coverage

Eligibility hinges on specific group characteristics and regulatory standards, ensuring a bona fide connection between members and the policyholder, typically an employer. Regulations define acceptable group sizes and necessary participation rates, directly influencing the group's qualification for insurance offerings.

13.4 Marketing of Group Health Plans

Effective marketing adheres to stringent regulatory standards while addressing the unique needs of the target group. Strategies vary significantly based on the plan's delivery setting, emphasizing clarity, accuracy, and relevance to the prospective members' needs.

13.5 Employer-Sponsored Group Health Plans

Employer-sponsored plans vary greatly, influenced by company size, employee needs, and legal mandates. Design factors such as deductibles, copays, and covered services are tailored to balance employee needs with financial realities. The administrative intricacies, including benefits coordination and response to employment changes, require meticulous management to ensure regulatory compliance and participant satisfaction.

13.6 Small Employer Group Health Plans

These plans cater to the unique needs of small businesses, adhering to regulations designed to ensure fairness and accessibility. Legal mandates cover a range of stipulations, from coverage mandates to pricing models, significantly impacting plan structure and availability.

13.7 Regulation of Group Health Insurance

The regulatory environment for group health insurance encompasses a complex web of state and federal laws. These regulations address a multitude of aspects, from participant eligibility to coverage parameters, shaping the landscape in which group plans operate. An understanding of the interplay between group insurance and Medicare is particularly critical, as it informs coverage options for older employees and those transitioning into retirement.

13.8 Expanding on the Essentials

The significance of group health insurance extends beyond simple coverage; it's a tool for businesses to attract and retain talent while ensuring the well-being of their workforce. The intricacies of policy design, legal compliance, and cost management are central themes in the creation and maintenance of these plans. As the healthcare landscape evolves, so too do the strategies for managing group health benefits, underscoring the need for ongoing education and adaptation by businesses and insurance professionals alike.

13.9 Advanced Considerations in Group Health Insurance

Beyond basic features, group health insurance encompasses advanced considerations such as wellness programs, mental health coverage, and telemedicine services. These elements reflect a holistic approach to employee well-being and are increasingly important in modern benefit packages. Additionally, the role of technology in administering benefits, from online enrollment platforms to digital health records, represents a significant shift in how group health plans operate and engage with members.

Case Study Title: Navigating Network Changes in a Large Employer's Health Plan

Background:

A large corporation, ABC Inc., decides to change its health insurance provider to offer better rates and updated services.

Scenario:

ABC Inc. must transition its 500 employees to the new network without disrupting ongoing treatments and maintaining employee morale.

Policy Details:

The new health plan offers a narrower network but better preventive care options.

Action Taken:

ABC Inc. communicates the changes through a series of meetings, provides comparison charts, and sets up a hotline for employee questions.

Outcome:

The transition sees a 90% retention rate, with most employees satisfied with the new options.

Conclusion:

Proactive communication and support are key to successfully transitioning group health plans.

Discussion Points for Insurance Exam Preparation:

- Strategies for evaluating and communicating network changes to employees.
- Best practices for transitioning between health plans with minimal disruption.
- The importance of employee feedback in selecting and implementing new health plans.

Frequently Asked Questions:

1. How do group health plans benefit from experience rating?

Experience rating allows premiums to be adjusted based on the specific claims history of the group, potentially lowering costs for groups with healthier populations.

2. What should employers consider when offering group health insurance?

Employers should evaluate employee needs, budget constraints, regulatory obligations, and the potential impacts on employee satisfaction and retention.

3. How are small employer group health plans regulated?

Small employer plans are regulated to ensure

Chapter 14: Fundamentals of Dental Insurance

14.1 Introduction to Dental Insurance

Dental insurance stands as a pivotal component of comprehensive health care strategies, aimed specifically at facilitating access to vital dental treatments. This type of insurance is not only instrumental in providing financial relief for dental care expenses but also plays a significant role in promoting oral health and, by extension, the overall well-being of individuals. A profound understanding of the range and extent of dental treatments covered by various insurance plans is indispensable. Such knowledge ensures that individuals can fully leverage their benefits while fostering a holistic approach to oral health care.

Dental insurance plans are structured to encompass a wide variety of treatments, each tailored to meet different aspects of oral health maintenance and care. The spectrum of covered services typically includes:

- Diagnostic Services: This category encompasses initial examinations, X-rays, and other diagnostic measures essential for identifying oral health issues.

- Preventive Services: Aimed at thwarting dental diseases, these services include regular cleanings, application of fluoride treatments, and the placement of sealants to prevent tooth decay.

- Restorative Services: These services are integral for repairing damaged teeth and include procedures like fillings, crowns, and bridges, crucial for restoring dental health and functionality.

- Oral Surgery: This includes a range of surgical procedures such as tooth extractions and gum surgery, necessary for addressing more severe oral health issues.

- Endodontics: A specialized sector focusing on treatments related to the dental pulp and root, including root canal therapy, vital for preserving natural teeth.

- Periodontics: Pertains to the treatment of gum-related diseases and conditions, emphasizing the health of the supporting structures of the teeth.

- Prosthodontics: This area covers the creation and fitting of artificial replacements for missing teeth, including dentures, bridges, and implants, crucial for restoring and maintaining normal oral function and appearance.

- Orthodontics: Dedicated to rectifying alignment issues of teeth and jaws, employing braces and other orthodontic devices to ensure proper alignment and function.

The multi-faceted nature of these categories underscores the critical need for comprehensive dental insurance that covers a broad spectrum of oral health services, from preventative measures to more intricate surgical and restorative procedures.

Dental Indemnity Plans, commonly recognized as traditional dental insurance, stand out for their flexibility regarding the choice of dental care providers. These plans are distinctly marked by:

- Structured Benefit Categories: They typically segregate services into diagnostic/preventive, basic, and major categories, each with specific coverage rates, thereby prioritizing preventive care to encourage regular dental visits.

- Varied Coverage Levels: Coverage rates differ across categories, with preventive services generally receiving higher coverage to promote regular dental check-ups and maintenance.

- Deductibles and Coinsurance: These features require patients to pay an initial amount (the deductible) before the insurance kicks in and to share a portion of the costs (coinsurance), promoting responsible utilization of dental services.

- Combination Plans: Some plans integrate features from various types of dental insurance, blending provider choice flexibility with cost-efficiency.

- Plan Exclusions and Limitations: These are commonplace, setting waiting periods for specific treatments, service frequency caps, and exclusions for conditions pre-dating coverage.

- Predetermination of Benefits: This process is advocated for expensive treatments; the insurer assesses and approves cost estimates before services are provided, clarifying coverage and reducing uncertainties for both the patient and the dental care provider.

Grasping the nuances of dental indemnity plans is essential for individuals aiming to navigate their dental care options effectively. It ensures they are well-informed about their coverage specifics, enabling them to make educated decisions regarding their oral health care while managing their financial contributions prudently. By comprehensively understanding these aspects, individuals can optimize their dental care experiences, ensuring they receive necessary treatments without undue financial strain.

14.2 Group Dental Expense Plans in the Workplace

Group dental plans in the workplace are an essential component of employee benefits packages, enhancing overall employee satisfaction and well-being. These plans can be structured in various ways, impacting both the employer's cost and the benefits available to employees:

- Integrated Deductibles vs. Stand-Alone Dental Plans: Integrated deductibles combine the employee's medical and dental deductibles, potentially increasing dental care usage by reducing out-of-pocket costs. In contrast, stand-alone dental plans have separate deductibles, which may result in lower immediate out-of-pocket costs for dental care but higher overall expenses before benefits kick in.

- Minimizing Adverse Selection: Employers can minimize adverse selection, where only those expecting dental expenses opt-in, by mandating participation or offering the dental plan as part of a standard benefits package. This spreads the risk across a larger group, keeping premiums more manageable for all employees.

- Design and Effectiveness Factors: Several factors influence the design and effectiveness of group dental plans, including the scope of coverage, choice of in-network versus out-of-network providers, co-payment structures, and annual maximum benefits. Plans must balance comprehensiveness with affordability to meet the diverse needs of employees while staying within the employer's budget.

Case Study: Implementing a New Group Dental Plan at Tech Innovations Inc.

Background:

Tech Innovations Inc. decided to introduce a new group dental plan to enhance its benefits package.

Scenario:

The HR department noticed low dental care utilization among employees due to high out-of-pocket costs.

Policy Details:

The new plan features lower deductibles, expanded in-network options, and increased annual maximum benefits.

Action Taken:

HR conducted comprehensive employee education sessions and provided detailed comparisons between old and new plans.

Outcome:

Increased enrollment in the dental plan and higher employee satisfaction were observed.

Conclusion:

Effective communication and understanding employees' needs are crucial for successful implementation.

Discussion Points for Insurance Exam Preparation:

- Assessing employee needs to tailor dental benefits effectively.

- Strategies for communicating changes and benefits to employees.

- The impact of plan design on utilization and employee satisfaction.

Frequently Asked Questions:

1. What distinguishes group dental plans from individual dental insurance?

Group dental plans are typically part of an employee benefits package, offering coverage at reduced rates due to the lower risk for insurers spread across a large group. In contrast, individual dental plans are purchased privately and can be more costly due to higher risk and administrative costs.

2. How can employers minimize adverse selection in dental plans?

Employers can minimize adverse selection by offering dental insurance as a mandatory part of their benefits package or by providing incentives for employees to enroll, thus ensuring that a broader range of individuals, not just those expecting dental procedures, participates.

3. What factors should be considered when designing a group dental plan?

Employers should consider factors such as coverage levels, deductibles, co-payments, choice of providers, and whether orthodontic and cosmetic procedures are covered. They should also consider the specific needs of their workforce and the competitiveness of their benefits package.

4. How do integrated deductibles differ from stand-alone dental deductibles?

Integrated deductibles combine the employee's medical and dental deductibles, which may encourage more preventative care by reducing total out-of-pocket expenses. Stand-alone dental deductibles are separate from medical deductibles, which may lead to lower initial costs for dental care but higher overall expenses before insurance coverage begins.

Chapter 15: Insurance for Senior Citizens and Special Needs Individuals

Insurance for senior citizens and individuals with special needs encompasses a range of plans designed specifically to address the healthcare and financial needs peculiar to these groups. This insurance plays a pivotal role in managing the costs associated with aging and specialized healthcare needs, ensuring that these vulnerable sections of the population have access to necessary medical treatments without the burden of exorbitant expenses.

15.1 Understanding Medicare

Medicare is a cornerstone of senior healthcare in the United States, structured to provide comprehensive coverage to its beneficiaries:

- Eligibility and Enrollment: Beyond the standard age and health condition requirements, understanding the specific enrollment periods and conditions can prevent lapses in coverage and avoid penalties.

- Coverage and Benefits: Each Medicare part covers different aspects of healthcare, from hospital stays under Part A to outpatient services under Part B, and it's crucial to understand the scope and limitations of each to optimize benefits.

- Costs and Premiums: Costs associated with Medicare, including premiums, deductibles, and copayments, can significantly impact financial planning. Beneficiaries need to budget for these expenses and understand how they can change annually.

Supplementary Coverage: Recognizing the gaps in Medicare coverage is essential for seniors to seek additional policies like Medigap or Medicare Advantage Plans, which can provide broader healthcare coverage and reduce out-of-pocket costs.

15.2 Medicare Supplement Plans

These plans are integral for those seeking to fill the gaps left by Original Medicare. Understanding the nuances of these plans can aid consumers in making informed choices:

- Choice and Flexibility: With various standardized plans available, individuals can select the supplement coverage that best suits their healthcare needs and financial situation.

- Consumer Protections: Certain states have unique regulations and consumer protections related to Medigap policies. Being aware of these can help individuals make safer, more informed decisions.

- Plan Comparison: Comparing different Medigap plans and understanding the specific benefits of each, including coverage for foreign travel emergencies and excess charges, is crucial for selecting the most appropriate supplementary coverage.

15.3 Alternative Coverage for Medicare Beneficiaries

Exploring alternative coverage options can provide additional security and benefits:

- Integration with Other Plans: Understanding how Medicare works with other insurance plans, such as employer-sponsored health plans or Medicaid, can help beneficiaries maximize their coverage and minimize costs.

- Special Needs Plans: These are tailored for individuals with particular diseases or characteristics and can offer specialized coverage that better meets their health needs.

15.4 Long-Term Care Insurance

This type of insurance is increasingly important as the population ages, covering services that Medicare does not:

- Comprehensive Coverage: Delving into the types of services covered, such as in-home care, assisted living, and nursing home care, helps individuals plan for potential future needs.

- Policy Choices: Evaluating different policies based on coverage, elimination periods, and benefit duration can guide consumers in choosing a plan that aligns with their long-term care needs and financial resources.

- State Partnerships: Some states offer Long-Term Care Partnership Programs, which allow individuals to protect a portion of their assets while qualifying for Medicaid, should their long-term care needs extend beyond their policy benefits.

Case Study: Comprehensive Care Planning for Mrs. Johnson

Background:

Mrs. Johnson, an 80-year-old widow with a chronic condition, is assessing her healthcare coverage.

Scenario:

She is considering a transition from Original Medicare to a Medicare Advantage Plan for broader coverage.

Policy Details:

Mrs. Johnson's current plan includes Medicare Parts A and B, with a separate prescription drug plan.

Action Taken:

She compared Medicare Advantage options, considering network restrictions, additional benefits, and out-of-pocket costs.

Outcome:

Mrs. Johnson chose a Medicare Advantage Plan that offers comprehensive coverage, including additional wellness programs.

Conclusion:

Thorough comparison and understanding of available Medicare options enabled Mrs. Johnson to select a plan that best suits her healthcare needs and financial situation.

Discussion Points for Insurance Exam Preparation:

- Understanding the differences and similarities between Original Medicare and Medicare Advantage.

- Evaluating the long-term benefits and drawbacks of switching from Original Medicare to a Medicare Advantage Plan.

- Assessing the impact of changing healthcare needs on Medicare plan selection.

Frequently Asked Questions:

1. How does one navigate the transition from Original Medicare to Medicare Advantage?

Research and compare different Medicare Advantage plans, considering factors like coverage, costs, and provider networks.

2. What are the considerations for enrolling in a Medigap policy after the open enrollment period?

After the open enrollment period, you may be subject to medical underwriting, and acceptance is not guaranteed. Compare costs and coverage options carefully.

3. How can individuals with special needs ensure they are getting the right coverage under Medicare?

They should evaluate their specific health needs, review the Special Needs Plans available, and consider consulting with a Medicare advisor.

4. What should seniors know about the costs associated with Medicare Part D?

Seniors should understand the Part D premium, deductible, copayments, and the coverage gap to effectively budget for prescription drug costs.

5. How can beneficiaries protect themselves from Medicare fraud?

Be cautious of unsolicited requests for Medicare numbers, review Medicare statements closely, and report any suspicious activities.

6. What are the key benefits of long-term care insurance for seniors?

It provides coverage for extended care services that Medicare does not cover, helping to protect savings and assets from high long-term care costs.

Chapter 16: Federal Tax Considerations for Health Insurance

16.1 Introduction to Tax Considerations for Health Insurance

Understanding federal tax implications associated with health insurance is crucial for both personal and business planning. Different types of health insurance have varying tax impacts, influencing decisions on coverage options and financial planning. It's essential for individuals and business owners to comprehend these tax aspects to optimize their health insurance benefits and minimize tax liabilities.

16.2 Tax Aspects of Personally-Owned Health Insurance

Health insurance can have significant tax implications, especially when it comes to disability income, medical expenses, and long-term care insurance:

- Disability Income Insurance: Generally, if you pay the premiums for disability income insurance, any benefits received are tax-free. However, if your employer pays for the insurance, the benefits may be taxable.

- Medical Expense Insurance: Premiums for medical expense insurance are typically tax-deductible if they, along with other medical expenses, exceed a certain percentage of your adjusted gross income.

- Long-Term Care Insurance: Premiums can be deductible depending on your age and the policy's qualifications. Benefits received from a qualified long-term care insurance policy are generally tax-free up to a certain limit.

- Settlement Options: The choice of settlement option can impact the tax treatment of insurance benefits, especially when it comes to life insurance policies used for medical expenses.

16.3 Employer-Provided Group Health Insurance Taxation

Employer-provided health benefits offer significant tax advantages:

- Non-Taxable Benefits: Generally, health insurance premiums paid by an employer are not taxable to the employee and are deductible by the employer.

- Disability Income: If an employer provides disability income insurance, the premiums are not considered taxable income to the employee, but any benefits received are taxable if the employer paid the premiums.

- Medical and Dental Expenses: These are typically excluded from taxable income when paid for by the employer.

- Accidental Death and Dismemberment: Premiums paid by the employer are not taxable to the employee, but benefits may be subject to tax.

- Medical Expense Coverage for Self-Employed Individuals

- Self-employed individuals can deduct 100% of their health insurance premiums from their taxable income, including premiums for medical, dental, and long-term care insurance, under certain conditions.

16.4 Business Disability Insurance Tax Implications

Business-related disability insurance, such as key person insurance or buy-sell agreement funding policies, has distinct tax implications:

- Key Person Disability Income: Premiums are not deductible as a business expense, but benefits received are typically tax-free.

- Buy-Sell Policies: Premiums are not tax-deductible, and benefits used to buy out a disabled partner's interest are not taxable.

16.5 Implications of the Affordable Care Act (ACA) on Taxes

The ACA introduced several tax-related provisions affecting individuals and businesses:

- Premium Tax Credits: Available to individuals and families to lower the cost of insurance coverage purchased through the Health Insurance Marketplace.

- Business Tax Credits: Small businesses providing health insurance may qualify for tax credits to offset costs.

- Medicare Tax Increase: High-income individuals may see an increase in their Medicare taxes.

Case Study: Navigating Tax Implications for a Small Business

Background:

A small business owner is reassessing their health insurance offerings in light of new tax laws.

Scenario:

The business offers group health insurance and is considering adding a qualified small employer health reimbursement arrangement (QSEHRA).

Policy Details:

The plan provides standard health coverage, with the addition of the new QSEHRA.

Action Taken:

The owner consulted with a tax advisor to understand the tax benefits and implications.

Outcome:

The business optimized its health insurance offerings while maximizing tax advantages.

Conclusion:

Understanding the tax implications of health insurance decisions is crucial for business planning.

Discussion Points for Insurance Exam Preparation:

- How do different types of health insurance impact tax liabilities for businesses and individuals?

- What are the tax benefits of employer-provided health insurance under current laws?

- How do changes in health insurance laws, such as the ACA, affect tax planning for individuals and businesses?

Frequently Asked Questions:

1. How are health insurance premiums treated in personal tax filings?

For individuals, health insurance premiums can often be deducted if total medical expenses exceed a certain percentage of adjusted gross income. For the self-employed, premiums can be directly deducted.

2 Are employer contributions to employee health insurance plans taxable?

Employer contributions are generally not taxable to the employee and are deductible by the employer.

3. What tax implications should be considered when choosing between different health insurance plans?

Consider the deductibility of premiums, the taxation of benefits, and any applicable tax credits or penalties.

4. How do the ACA's provisions impact individual tax liabilities?

They can affect individuals through premium tax credits, penalties for not having insurance, and additional Medicare taxes for high earners.

5. Can long-term care insurance premiums be deducted on taxes?

Yes, within certain limits based on age and if the policy qualifies under IRS rules.

6. What are the tax implications for small businesses offering health insurance?

Small businesses may qualify for tax credits, and premiums paid on behalf of employees are typically deductible as a business expense.

Your Next Steps - Equipping Your Journey to Success and Taking Flight

Congratulations! You've reached the culmination of this comprehensive study guide, written to empower you on your path towards becoming a licensed life and health insurance professional. While the specific content and format of your state's licensing exams may differ slightly, the foundational knowledge explored in this book remains universally applicable.

Remember:

Embrace lifelong learning: The insurance landscape is constantly evolving. Stay current with regulatory changes, emerging trends, and new product offerings. Utilize resources like the National Association of Insurance Commissioners (NAIC) and your state's insurance department website to remain informed.

Commit to continuing education: Maintaining your license necessitates ongoing professional development. Continuing education courses not only fulfill licensing requirements but also provide valuable opportunities to enhance your expertise and adapt to industry advancements.

Uphold ethical conduct: Integrity and professionalism are cornerstones of the insurance industry. Always prioritize client needs, act with fairness and honesty, and maintain confidentiality of entrusted information.

Beyond the Exams:

Passing your exams unlocks the door to a rewarding career safeguarding the financial security and well-being of individuals and families. You'll become a trusted advisor, helping clients navigate complex insurance options, make informed decisions, and ensure their financial preparedness for various life events. Remember, the knowledge and skills acquired through this guide will not only equip you to excel on the exams but also serve as a strong foundation for a fulfilling career in this dynamic industry.

Take Flight with Confidence:

Now, it's time to put your knowledge to the test by practising with the 300 exam questions that come with this book. These questions will help you assess your strengths and weaknesses, and prepare you for the real exam. You can access them by scanning the QR code at the front of the book with your smartphone or tablet.

These questions, mirroring the format and difficulty level of the actual exam, offer an invaluable opportunity to:

- Solidify your understanding: Apply acquired knowledge to real-world scenarios presented in the practice questions.

- Identify areas for improvement: Pinpoint topics requiring further review and focus your study efforts accordingly.

- Sharpen critical thinking skills: Analyze questions meticulously, evaluate answer choices thoughtfully, and justify your selected responses.

- Boost exam confidence: Regularly engaging with practice questions enhances your test-taking skills, speed, and overall exam preparedness.

By actively engaging with the practice test questions and leveraging the diverse resources available, you'll confidently take flight towards a successful career in life and health insurance. Remember, success is not a one-time event, but a continuous journey of learning and improvement. The more you practice, the more confident and ready you will be. Use the QR code to access the practice test questions and get started today. Good luck!

Download All your Practice Tests With This QR Code or Follow This Link:

https://book-bonus.com/life-and-health-insurance/